Using Statistics

Using Statistics: A Gentle Introduction

Gordon Rugg

 Open University Press

Open University Press
McGraw-Hill Education
McGraw-Hill House
Shoppenhangers Road
Maidenhead
Berkshire
England
SL6 2QL

email: enquiries@openup.co.uk
world wide web: www.openup.co.uk

and Two Penn Plaza, New York, NY 10121-2289, USA

First published 2007

A catalogue record of this book is available from the British Library

ISBN-13: 978 0 335 22218 6 (pb)   978 0 335 22219 3 (hb)
ISBN-10: 0 335 22218 8 (pb)   0 335 22219 6 (hb)

Library of Congress Cataloguing-in-Publication Data
CIP data applied for

Typeset by RefineCatch Limited, Bungay, Suffolk
Printed in Poland by OZGraf S.A
www.polskabook.pl

The McGraw-Hill Companies

Contents

List of figures

Preamble

Some [. . .] literati with whom I discussed the matter were at first shocked by or contemptuous of my audacity in declaring that I intended to bring out a simple version . . .

(*I Ching: The Book of Change*, p. 17)

So there you are, contemplating the prospect of having to use statistics. If you're a normal human being, then it's not a tempting prospect. For most people, reading about statistics is like the time they tried teaching themselves chess from a book. The first page says what all the pieces are, and what the rules are; it helpfully explains that the one looking like a nice horsey is the knight. Two pages later the author is deep in a description of the Refused Capablanca Gambit, and the average reader is utterly lost and confused. Introductory stats courses can be even more dispiriting. They're typically taught by statisticians whose brains appear to be wired up differently from yours, and by the end of week two you're feeling like a delinquent sailor being dragged through heavy surf on a hatch cover as punishment for your sins, struggling just to keep your head above water, with no chance of seeing any bigger picture of things.

Most people emerge from their first encounter with stats feeling distinctly bruised, and with a mental image of stats as a bizarre set of meaningless rituals that you have to follow because you're told to, but which are of no real use to you. The trouble is that even the best introductory stats courses don't have enough time to work through both the big picture and the nuts and bolts of statistics, so students end up with a shaky edifice of knowledge built on thin foundations. Traditional stats books tend to focus on the tests themselves, and on the maths underlying them, as opposed to the issue of why you might want to use them as part of your research, and how you can use them to help answer your research questions. Many books do a very good job of describing statistics from the viewpoint of statistics. This is fine if you're a statistics student, but a bit much to grasp if you're just doing a stats module on a psychology or biology course, and particularly awkward if you're not very comfortable with maths. Statistics books are also typically strong on logical, efficient layout, and not quite so strong on readability, excitement, mystery and the like.

There are also guidebooks for various stats software packages, which are fine as a guide to the relevant package, but not so fine for seeing what the underlying concepts are or for seeing how those concepts link up with other important parts of research, such as choosing a research design or a data analysis method. When you try using the package, you typically have to choose between lots of options which you don't really understand, after which it spits out a long set of figures which look very precise, but which mean absolutely nothing to you: it's horribly tempting to cut and paste them into your write-up, and hope miserably that nobody asks awkward questions about whether you used the right test in the first place.

There is at least one brilliant exception to this woeful set of generalisations, in the form of Darrell Huff's book *How to Lie with Statistics*. It's crystal-clear, it gives the big picture as well as describing the nuts and bolts, and it's so well written that you can read it for entertainment. Unfortunately, it only covers a subset of statistics, and in the half century since Huff wrote it, nobody as far as I know has done the same for the rest of statistics. Modesty forbids claiming that I've finished the job that Huff started, but I have had a crack at it.

This book is intended to provide an overview of statistics, and to explain how statistics fit into the big picture of research, with particular attention to using statistics as part of a coherent research design. It also describes the concepts on which statistics are based, to give you some idea of what's going on in a given test. When a new concept makes its first appearance, it's shown in bold italics, as a signal that it's a technical term. I've explained various bits of the maths where necessary, but have tried not to go overboard on this. On the same basis, I've not given the formulae for working out most tests, since most people use a stats package to do the calculations, so they never see the formulae. If you feel the praiseworthy desire to do the calculations by hand, there are references at the back of the book to a few classic stats books, which contain the formulae for large numbers of statistical tests. Similarly, there's not much about individual stats packages, for which good guides are available. That's left more space for explaining the underlying concepts, and for illustrating them with improving tales and assorted metaphors.

To provide some variety, each chapter begins with a quotation. There is no need to read the original sources of these quotations, since some of them are the product of misspent youth; tales of eldritch horror about elder gods and albino werewolves are unlikely to bring a good night's sleep. All the anecdotes, however improbable, are faithfully reported, though some of the 'friend of a colleague' stories may originally be urban legends.

I hope that you will find this book enjoyable and useful.

Acknowledgements

To render just praise to the gallant conduct and impetuous attack of Mr Dillon,
I am perfectly unequal to.

(*Master and Commander*, p. 326)

I am grateful to many people for their help with this book. I would particularly like to acknowledge Wynford Bellin and Elizabeth Gaffan for the help they gave when I was first learning statistics. Barbara Kitchenham, Helen Urwin and Alexandra Lamont gave invaluable help in the preparation of this book. Any errors in this book are my fault, not theirs. I would also like to thank Sue Gerrard for her help with the manuscript.

1

Some introductory concepts

...a wretched character, who had been ostracised, not because anyone was afraid of his power and prestige, but because he was a thoroughly bad lot and a disgrace to the city.

(*History of the Peloponnesian War*, p. 580)

Learning statistics is a bit like learning wilderness survival. Discovering how to survive in an Arctic blizzard is all very well if you enjoy that sort of thing. Similarly, if you've chosen to do a statistics degree, then you're likely to appreciate the beauty of an elegant equation or a challenging bit of measurement theory. It's different, however, if you're an easy-going indoor type of person by inclination, but are having an unintended learning experience with snowdrifts and wind chill after your car breaks down one January night, miles from the nearest habitation. Many students first encounter statistics in a similar way: one day they are happily studying Biology 101, savouring the joys of nature, and then they are suddenly thrown into the Statistics for Biologists module, whether they like it or not, on the grounds that it's good for them and on the syllabus. Explaining that you're not very good at sums or that you're scared of maths will not get you far. At best, you might receive a sympathetic word before being thrown back into the module; at worst, you might receive an improving homily which is the statistical equivalent of being told about the woman who survived a plane crash in the Sierra Nevada in midwinter and walked through the snow for thirty-six hours to civilisation. In high-heeled fashion boots. With a broken arm. It may be true, but it's unlikely to help your morale or your attitude towards statistics.

If you view statistics as something unconnected with the rest of the world, then your experiences are likely to be uninspiring at best, and depressingly frustrating at worst. It's much the same if you view statistics as a set of recipes which you have to memorise without understanding them. If, however, you work backwards from what statistics are used for in research, then it all starts to make much more sense.

The reason has its origins in history. Research is about finding answers to questions. Some questions can be answered without using numbers, and there is a long and honourable tradition of doing this. Suppose, for instance, that you were an ancient Athenian being taught by Socrates, and that some syco-phantic creep of a student claimed that Socrates was immortal because of his wisdom. You could respond by using logic, with no numbers involved, point-ing out that Socrates was a man, and that all men are mortal, therefore Socrates was mortal. Whether this would get you a better grade in his next test is another question, but it would answer the question elegantly and concisely.

Other questions require a different type of evidence to give an answer. Sup-pose, for instance, that someone starts an argument about the shape of horses' teeth. You can't find the answer to this question by just using logic; the answer has to come from observation, which in this case would involve observing the contents of a horse's mouth.

You can answer quite a lot of research questions using a combination of logic and observation, but you can't handle every problem this way. There are many problems which involve a chain of reasoning which looks logical, but which is clearly not quite right. For example, Zeno's paradox involves an archer and a target. Before the archer's arrow can hit the target, it has to travel half-way to the target. That sounds fair and reasonable. Before it can travel half-way, though, it has to travel a quarter of the way. Again, fair and reasonable. Before it can travel a quarter of the way, it has to travel an eighth of the way, and you now begin to realise where the reasoning is going. Since you can subdivide the distance an infinite number of times, you can go on forever subdividing it, so the arrow never gets the chance to move, therefore movement is impossible.

There's something wrong in the reasoning, since movement clearly is pos-sible, but where is the error? It took more than two thousand years before someone showed where the error was, and it involved some heavy theory about the nature of infinity. If the conclusion of that chain of reasoning hadn't been so obviously silly, would anyone have spotted that there was an error in the reasoning? And how many other chains of reasoning with sensible-looking conclusions do we accept unquestioningly, which might have equally huge gaps in their logic hiding deep beneath their placid surface? It's not an encouraging thought.

Observation also has drawbacks and limits. Imagine, for instance, that a traveller from a distant land tells you a story about having seen a crocodile give birth to live young, rather than laying eggs in the usual manner. How could you check the accuracy of this account? Observing thousands of other croco-diles wouldn't help much, since what is at issue is the particular crocodile he saw. Even if you found that crocodile, and it laid eggs every year for the rest of its life with never a live birth in sight, the traveller could still claim that it had given birth to live young when he was watching it, and that the later observations were irrelevant.

Leaving pregnant crocodiles to one side for the moment, there are other types of question which can't be answered even by the most scrupulously honest logic and observation. Suppose that you are living in Tudor England, and are unfortunate enough to contract smallpox. The doctor proposes to treat you by, among other things, draping the room in red cloth. (Yes, some of them actually did this.) You ask why he proposes the red cloth, and he tells you that it worked for his last patient. This sounds distinctly questionable to you, but you don't have much to lose, so you go along with it. After your recovery, the doctor adds you to his list of successful cures with red cloth. You might point out that a lot of other people also recovered from smallpox without any red cloth, but you're aware that in addition to sounding a bit ungrateful, it's also not the strongest of arguments in its present form. How could you improve it?

One way is to look at the cure rates. If the rate of recovery among the red cloth patients is no different from the cure rate among patients who didn't go through the red cloth experience, then the obvious implication is that the red cloth didn't make any difference. That's fine if the two rates are exactly the same. What, though, if the rates are slightly different but not enormously different? If you've spent a lot of time gathering the information about the recovery rates, and then realised that you don't know what to do with it, you might understandably feel rather vexed. A common strategy in research is to work backwards from your goal – imagine that you've found the answer to your question, and then ask yourself what form that answer would take, and also ask yourself what you would do with that answer. It's a wise strategy, and one to which we will return later. This example also illustrates the point that it's possible to find supporting evidence for more or less any assertion, so supporting evidence by itself isn't usually much use for getting insights into a question; what's more useful is knowing which evidence will allow you to eliminate one or more of the possibilities. That's another theme to which we return later.

This, traditionally, is the point at which writers of stats books come up with a rhetorical flourish, and break into an improving lecture about the glories of statistics. You'll probably experience enough of these to satisfy anyone before you finish your course, so we'll skip the conventional lecture, and start preparing for the next section. The next section, as you have doubtless guessed, is a gentle walk through some questions which can be answered using numbers of one form or another.

With the space saved by omitting the paean, we can cover another topic, namely the roles of Bad People and Cynical Readers in academic life. As a student, you may be blissfully unaware that there are people who misuse statistics deliberately. Academic staff have usually witnessed more than enough such sin to last anyone a long lifetime. In consequence, they are usually cynical when reading students' work. If you write something which gives the impression that you are a Bad Person, then a Cynical Reader is likely to start looking very closely at what you've done, to assess whether you're actually a sinner (and therefore a potential case for an academic misconduct hearing) or just clueless (and therefore a potential case for a bad mark). Conversely, if you send out signals in your writing which show clearly that you're a virtuous and well-informed student, then your chances of a happy ending and a good mark are much higher. The things which send out good and bad signals are well known to academics, but there's a general presumption that it's the students' job to work most of these out for themselves, which can be a bit trying if you're attempting to do a degree and have some shreds of life at the same time. I've therefore flagged these things explicitly where they're mentioned, so that you can send out the right signals. There's also a list of classic problematic phrasings in Table A.2 in the Appendix.

Right, on to a gentle stroll through the next topic, namely some basic concepts in descriptive statistics.

Describing what you've found

Some research questions can be answered, and answered well, without measuring or counting anything. Suppose, for instance, that you're tracing the spread of the concept of the noble savage, via mentions in literature. You could do it brilliantly without using a single number apart from the publication dates of the literature. More often, though, you'll be aware that your question could be answered better with numbers of some sort. Suppose that you're investigating hassles affecting students and their academic performance. You could simply list the hassles that you uncover via masterful use of projective questionnaires and indirect observation, but that would raise obvious questions, such as how many people mentioned each hassle, or how serious they considered each hassle to be. It's easy to get some numbers in answer to these questions (though we'll ignore for the moment the issue of how to get answers that bear some relation to reality). Once you've got some findings about your hassles, or the arthropods you've found on a windswept hillside, or whatever it is you're studying, then you are the proud possessor of some data, and you'll need to describe that data.

If you're describing your data, what do you need to describe, and why? One answer is that you need to describe the things which assure a Cynical Reader that you are not a sinful person presenting a heavily edited version of events. This section discusses these things, what sinful people do, what basic descriptive statistics involve, and how basic descriptive statistics can contribute something positive to your life. We will return to descriptive statistics later in more detail, after clearing some other ground.

What have you got?

In an ideal world, friends would always be trusty and true, virtue would always triumph, and you would always be able to trust completely whatever you read in print. The real world, however, is not quite like this: friends are only human, and sometimes let you down; virtue does not always triumph; and what you read may be a version of events which bears only a tangential relationship to reality. Suppose, for instance, that you have been investigating children's problems with learning mathematics, and you find that a particular theme keeps cropping up in their descriptions – for instance, misunderstanding fractions. You mention this in your write-up. What would an experienced reader think? They would probably wonder cynically whether your memory had helped the data along a bit, via selectively remembering only the handful of examples where the theme occurred and forgetting the majority where it didn't. Such things happen.

An obvious response to this is to give some figures to clarify the point. You could, for instance, mention that this theme was mentioned in 57.14% of cases. That looks pretty impressive, which is why percentages are a favourite way of misrepresenting data among sinful people. Why? In this example, 57.14% is suspiciously close to the percentage that you'd get if the theme was mentioned by four out of the seven pupils you studied. Four out of seven is not exactly the strongest set of data on which to build a theoretical edifice; four thousand out of seven thousand would be a very different proposition, but would produce the same percentage. This introduces the concept of sample size.

Sample size

One of the first things that Cynical Readers will wonder about, and which you therefore need to report so that you can pre-empt their suspicions, is how many instances you are reporting. This may be the number of pupils in your sample, or the number of people who completed your questionnaire, or the number of insects you found in one square metre of wet Welsh hillside on your ecology field trip. New researchers often have a touching faith that the bigger the sample, the better, but reality is a bit more complicated. With most research there comes a point of diminishing returns in **sample size**, where gathering more information doesn't tell you anything new. Gathering more data past this point is simply a waste of effort which could be better spent on other things. How do you know when you have reached this point? It's a good question, and one that we'll return to later.

So, at the end of this, the conclusion is that you tell the reader how big a sample you were using. If you're in a discipline which is strong on statistics and research design, then the convention is to call the number of cases n, for 'number'. If you had painstakingly collected thirty respondents, your write-up might therefore say something like '$n = 30$'. Laconic, but fine.

Extremes

Once you've told the reader how big your sample size is, the obvious next step is to tell them something about what's in the sample. One useful piece of information involves the extreme values in your sample – what the smallest value is, and what the biggest value is – so that the reader has some idea of the range within which your sample's values fall. Extreme values are another rich hunting ground for sinful people, which has given extreme values something of a bad name in some circles.

Suppose, for instance, that you see a claim that the Crowley Accelerated Learning System has improved learning by up to 78% in a sample of 4000 adults. This looks pretty impressive at first sight. What's wrong with it? A Cynical Reader will wonder what lies behind the words 'up to'. This might mean that most of the people in that sample improved quite a lot, with a fair number who improved by over 70%, and one who reached 78% improvement. It might, however, mean that one person showed that much improvement, and that none of the others showed any improvement whatsoever. That has very different implications for anyone wondering whether they should invest in the system.

The honest way to report your data is therefore to report the extreme values at both ends of the scale – the lowest as well as the highest.

This is not always as straightforward as it might appear, as illustrated by the case of the exasperated wombat. The case, as reported to me by a colleague, involved an Australian researcher who was performing classic behaviourist research into animal learning. Being a 'friend of a friend' story, it may be an urban legend, but it's a more memorable example than most properly documented and more mundane examples, so I'll use it anyway. The animals in the experiment pressed a lever, and every time they pressed the lever, they received some food; the research involved measuring how long it took animals to learn the association between lever-pressing and food. At the time, nobody had tried this on marsupials, so the researcher was keen to discover how marsupials compared with the usual suspects of rats, pigeons and suchlike. He therefore set up the equipment, put his wombat in the experimental cage, and started measuring. To his astonishment, once the wombat discovered the lever, it pressed the lever with a speed and persistence completely outside the range of values documented in all previous research. Understandably keen to see this prodigy in action, he abandoned the display screen and rushed over to the cage, where he discovered that the wombat, whose claws had grown considerably while in captivity and restrained from burrowing, had managed to get the lever stuck between two of its claws, and was shaking the lever in mounting exasperation in a vain bid to free itself, surrounded by a growing mound of disregarded food pellets.

Could you legitimately exclude such a case from your analysis, since it's clearly not a normal example? You almost certainly could in an extreme case like this, though you might brighten readers' lives by mentioning it somewhere in your write-up (and parenthetically claiming a brownie point for honestly reporting a case which you had decided to exclude from the analysis). Extreme values of this sort are known as **outliers**, and most disciplines have conventions about how to decide if something is an outlier, and about whether to exclude them. Less extreme examples can be more problematic. You might, for instance, have a small group of respondents whose scores are all much lower than the scores from the other respondents, suggesting that there is something different going on – perhaps, for example, the low-scoring respondents have misunderstood their instructions, or have taken a personal dislike to you and decided to sabotage their results. Can you exclude such cases? Probably not, but you might want to handle them by performing one analysis which includes the low-scoring respondents, and a separate analysis which excludes them, to see what difference this makes. One simple way of spotting potential outliers is to do a scattergram of your data (there's more about this in the section on patterns in data, a bit further on).

Means, modes and medians

Reporting your *n* and your extreme values is a good start, but still leaves much of the story untold. Suppose, for example, that you are on a zoology field trip, and you discover a group of unusually coloured limpets which appear also to be unusually large. This may be your chance to become a small legend in mollusc studies by identifying a new sub-species or even species, so you dutifully report the sizes of your limpets and compare them to a group of irreproachably normal limpets. To your chagrin, you discover that the group of normal limpets happens to include one specimen much larger than the others, and that your group of unusually coloured limpets happens to include one which is much smaller than the others. The consequence is that the number of specimens in the two groups is identical, and that the lowest and highest values in the two groups are also identical. Is all lost? No, because you can save the day by calculating the average size of the limpets in the two groups.

Averages are universally acknowledged to be a Good Thing – so good, in fact, that there are no less than three different types of average, each of which is calculated in a different way, and each of which can be misused by Bad People in different ways.

Means

The most widely known form of average is the ***mean***. This is so widely known that most ordinary mortals are unaware that there is any other form of average. You calculate the mean by adding together the values for each of your bits of data, and then dividing the total by the number of bits. The total is also known as the 'sum' – if you're short of space in a table, you can even abbreviate 'sum' by using the Greek character for 's', namely 'sigma', which looks like this in its capitalised form: Σ.

So, using a different example by way of a change, suppose you are studying stylistic development in the work of Barbara Cartland. You are particularly interested in comparing her minor works (e.g. *Cupid Rides Pillion*, from her Mod period) with her major works (e.g. *The Lady and the Highwayman*, from her historical romance period), using techniques based on something more systematic than subjective appreciation of literature, and you accordingly choose a random sample of five minor and five major works. As one of your measures of style, you decide to count how often she employs the literary device of dramatic prefiguration (where a minor event early in the story foreshadows a much more serious event of the same type later in the plot). The hypothetical results are as follows:

Minor works: 1, 4, 3, 5, 12 instances in each of the five books, respectively
Major works: 1, 9, 10, 9, 12 instances in each of the five books, respectively

Astonishingly, if you only look at the extreme values, then the two groups are indistinguishable: both have a lowest count of one instance, and a highest count of 12 instances. If we calculate the means, however, a very different picture emerges. For the minor works, the total score is 1+4+3+5+12, i.e. 25. If we divide this by the number of minor works, i.e. 5, the result is 25/5, i.e. 5. For the major works, however, the total score is 1+9+10+9+12, i.e. 40. If we divide this by the number of major works, i.e. 5, we obtain 41/5, i.e. 8.2. The conclusion, therefore, is that the mean scores for the two groups are different, with the minor works having a mean of 5 and the major works having a mean of 8.

Medians

That's one form of average. A second form is the **median**. If you line up a set of scores, from the smallest to the largest, then the median is the one which is in the middle of the line. Why should anyone have bothered to invent this form of average? The scores for the minor works provide an example of why medians can be useful. Most of the scores for the minor works are quite small, but there is one unusually high value of 12, which skews both the extreme score and also the mean. Without that solitary 12, the mean would be much lower. Means for smallish samples can easily be skewed by one or two abnormally large scores, something which is well known to practitioners of various professions where impression management is considered more important than giving the full story. Medians, however, are not particularly affected by the odd atypical score, so if you want to get a more realistic average from a rather patchy set of data, a median might give you a better picture.

If we take the scores above, and line them up from smallest to largest, we get the following lists:

Minor works: 1, 3, 4, 5, 12 instances
Major works: 1, 9, 9, 10, 12 instances

The median (i.e. the score in the middle) for the first list is 4, and the median for the second list is 9. The first of these, 4, is slightly lower than the mean for its group, since the mean is inflated a bit by the outlying score of 12. The second of these, 9, is slightly higher than the mean for its group, since the mean is dragged down by the outlying score of 1. The principle becomes still clearer if we imagine that the last figure for the first group was 112 instead of 12; the mean would then be 25, but the median would be unaffected by this, and would remain at 4.

Modes

The third form of average is the **mode**. The mode is the number which occurs most frequently in a list. In the case of the major works, for instance, there is one score of 1, there are two scores of 9, there is one score of 10 and there is one score of 12. The most frequently occurring score is therefore 9, with two occurrences. In the list of scores from the minor works each score is equally common, so there is no mode. Why should anyone care about modes, which can (particularly in small samples) look a bit haphazard? One reason is that modes can be useful for telling you whether your sample of data is all that it appears to be. Suppose, returning to our limpets, that you discover that one of your limpet groups shows two modes some distance apart from each other – for instance, 7 and 12 on your patented limpet size scale. This might be an indication that this data set actually consists of two different sorts of limpets which you have inadvertently lumped together – for instance, some nomadic limpets and some territorial limpets. If this is the case, then you'll need to do something about it, since otherwise your results will be little more than a work of fiction, which is not usually considered a good thing for results. We'll return to this theme later, when we discuss eyeballing data, and again when we discuss various statistical tests.

Variance and standard deviations

With the fictitious data above, an inquisitive reader might have noted that most of the data in each group clustered fairly closely together, and might have wondered whether it was possible to translate this impression into something more tangible, such as a number calculated to three decimal places. Such readers might be pleased to know that this can indeed be done, and might feel somewhat relieved to know that they don't need to do any mental arithmetic – calculators, spreadsheets and statistical packages will do it all for you. A particularly keen reader might wonder whether the process involves calculating some sort of average figure for how far each bit of data is from the mean; this is indeed the right general idea. It's one which turns up in all sorts of places later on in statistics, so we'll go into the underlying concepts here in some detail. The general idea is known as **measures of deviation**. If you're skimming through this book for the first time to get a general idea of how statistics can help your research, then you might choose to skip the details about how measures of deviation work, but it would be advisable to return to it later, once you're happy with the big picture. We'll work through the maths involved, to show how statistics often involves a simple calculation which is repeated to a tedious extent, but which is not conceptually difficult.

Sums of squares: a slight detour via a simpler path

One of the great English caves includes three main routes which potholers can follow. One is known as The Short Way; another is known as The Pretty Way; the last is known as The Dry Way. A similar principle applies to explaining measures of deviation, where there's a short way and a gentle way. The gentle way involves sums of squares. If you want to measure the amount of variation in your data, one simple way of doing it is to take the mean, and work out how far each individual score is from that mean. You can then add together the results from this, which will give you an overall measurement for how variable the individual scores are. That accounts for the 'sums' part of 'sums of squares'. There's another stage in the process, which involves squaring values, a subject to which we'll return in a moment. For the present, though, we'll start working through a simple example.

For the minor works of Barbara Cartland, the mean is 5, and the individual scores are 1, 3, 4, 5 and 12. If we subtract each of these in turn from the mean, the results are -4, -2, -1, 0 and 7.

In a simple world, we would simply add these together to obtain a figure for how far these numbers deviate from the mean. In the actual world, there is an apparent complication before we do any adding. The apparent complication is that 'sum of squares' is in fact short for 'sum of squared deviations from the mean'. As you might suspect, this means that we now square each of these numbers (i.e. multiply each one by itself). Why? There are various plausible answers. One is that it converts all the numbers into positive numbers, since otherwise when you added them all together, the negative numbers and positive numbers would all cancel each other out and leave you with a result of zero, as a necessary consequence of how the mean is defined. Another is that researchers, being on the whole liable to human frailty, might be inclined to depict their findings with whichever gloss is most favourable to their prejudices, so statisticians decided long ago to limit their own liabilities by making their tests as conservative and pessimistic as possible. Whichever of these is true, the outcome is the same: you multiply each of the newly derived numbers by itself. This has the immediately obvious outcome of making all the numbers positive; it also has the less immediately obvious outcome of emphasising any unusually large or small scores, which will emphasise any variability in your data. For the scores above (-4, -2, -1, 0 and 7) the results are as follows:

$$-4 \times -4 = 16$$
$$-2 \times -2 = 4$$
$$-1 \times -1 = 1$$

$$0 \times 0 = 0$$
$$7 \times 7 = 49$$
$$\text{total} = 70$$

This means that the sum of squared deviations from the mean for this group is 70. The corresponding figure for the other group (the major works) is almost identical, at 71.

You might at this stage be wondering whether it might be a good idea to un-square this total in some way, even if you're not quite sure why. It is indeed a good idea to take the square root of the total (we'd advise against using the phrase 'un-square' in front of mathematicians, who might not appreciate your sense of irony). The correct way to do this is a two-stage process. The first stage is used to allow for your sample size, since you could get the same value for a sum of squares from one small but incredibly variable set of data, or from a huge but incredibly consistent set of data. What you do is to take your sum of squares and divide it by your *n* (i.e. your sample size); the result from this is known as the **variance**.

The next stage is to calculate the square root of your variance. The resulting number is known as the **standard deviation**, a name which usually provokes at least one dubious witticism from immature or unkind students in a typical statistics class. Standard deviations turn out to be very useful in statistics, so I'll say a few words about them. (Mean variances don't crop up in many other places, for various reasons, so we'll leave them in peace for some time.)

Standard deviations

In the same way that averages are so useful that there are three types of them, so standard deviations are so useful that there are two types of them. The reason for this involves the familiar theme of taking a conservative view, to counteract any drive towards optimistic interpretation of the results.

Sometimes in research you have the luxury of working with a complete set of data – for instance, all the works of Virgil, or all the specimens of the Californian condor. (This is known technically as a **population**, which can be confusing to people who have already encountered the same term in the usual sense of 'people who live in a given country'.) More often, though, you have to work with a subset of whichever group you want to study: you want to know about all the limpets on the Dorset coast, but practicalities limit you to a subset consisting of the denizens of one rock pool, or you want to know about all primary school children, but you have to deal instead with the agents of chaos who populate one class in the local primary school. (This is known technically as a **sample**.) New researchers often agonise about the extent to which the results from their miniscule subset can be extrapolated to the complete population. To reduce this agonising a bit, statisticians helpfully developed the concept of having two measures of deviation from the mean, one intended for complete populations, and one intended for samples (i.e. subsets of the complete population). If you're dealing with a complete population, then you don't need to worry about extrapolation, since you already have the complete population, and you calculate the deviation in the way described above. The resulting number is described with the abbreviation σ, which is the Greek lower-case letter 's' and which can be remembered as short for 'standard deviation'.

If, on the other hand, you are dealing with a subset, then you use the more conservative version of standard deviation. This version involves a minor difference in what you do at the mean variance stage. Instead of dividing the sum of squares by your n (i.e. your sample size), you first subtract one from your n, to give you a slightly smaller number, and then divide the sum of squares by this slightly smaller number. You then un-square the result, as usual. Since you are dividing by a slightly smaller number, the outcome will be slightly larger than would otherwise be the case, and will produce a standard deviation which is a bit bigger than it would otherwise have been. So what? Looking at the mean and the standard deviation gives the reader an idea of how variable your data are, and of how much can be extrapolated from them. This version of the standard deviation errs on the side of making your data look more variable, which in turn makes you look like a sensible, moderate sort of person, not given to wildly enthusiastic ravings about the implications of your results (though a depressingly high proportion of new researchers will undo this good impression as soon as they return to connected prose in the 'discussion' section of their write-up). This version of standard deviation is usually represented by the abbreviation *sd*, short for 'standard deviation'. There's a tendency for Greek symbols to be used as abbreviations for measures relating to populations and for Latin characters to be used as abbreviations for measures relating to samples, but the full story is a bit more complex, and I'll resist the temptation to go into details.

What this can do for you

Much of the account above might convey a depressing impression of pitfalls to avoid, and risks of temptation. This section is intended to redress the balance, by discussing some of the ways in which statistics can make your life better.

One thing which statistics allow you to do is to move from subjective impressions towards something more tangible. If you can define the terms you are using to discuss something, then there's a fair chance that you can define them in a way that lets you measure something, and then you can collect data which let you answer some of those questions that you'd always been wondering about. (We'll tactfully not go into the implications of trying to discuss something if you can't define what you mean by your terms.) This process of turning a term into something you can measure is known technically as *operationalising your metrics*, which sounds technical enough to satisfy most people.

Another thing which statistics allow you to do is to identify things about your subject which you would probably miss otherwise. One example is the case of the hypothetical limpets, where the presence of two modes could alert you to the possibility that what you believed to be one group of limpets is actually two different groups, one consisting of a smallish variety of limpet and the other consisting of a larger variety of limpet. Another example is finding unexpected regularities or differences. Suppose, for instance, that you found that Barbara Cartland and William Shakespeare used almost identical frequencies of dramatic prefiguration in their writing. That would have implications for literary criticism; quite what those implications would be is an interesting question, but fortunately not one that falls within our scope.

That leads on to another, subtler thing that statistics can do for you. In some disciplines, there is a tradition of researchers advocating an argument, and defending it against all comers, using whatever supporting evidence comes to hand. Such disciplines do not usually feature a corresponding tradition of researchers gracefully accepting that the other side appears to be right, and withdrawing their own argument. This can cause understandable anxiety among researchers concerned about the risk of nailing their colours to a mast which is just about to sink beneath the waves. This risk can be elegantly avoided if you approach research from a viewpoint of inquiry (i.e. finding things out) rather than advocacy of the viewpoint that you had even before you saw any evidence. In the Cartland case, for instance, you might point out that one school of thought believes her to be stylistically much inferior to Shakespeare, whereas another school of thought argues that 'good writing' is purely a matter of conventional social taste. These viewpoints are mutually exclusive, so which one corresponds to reality? If the 'inferior style' view is right, then you would expect to find systematic differences between the two authors when you measured the features you used for defining 'good style'; if the 'social taste' view is right, then you would not expect to find any systematic differences between them. This phrasing means that you don't need to commit yourself to either viewpoint, and also means that whatever you find, it will be an interesting finding (though you might be well advised to start your career with some less controversial question).

On that note, we'll end this section. Descriptive statistics let you say what you've got, which can be unexpected and very interesting. Unfortunately, they don't tell you whether you've found something remarkable, or just something which has probably happened through random chance. You may find that there's a pattern in your data which looks very interesting, but that's not enough to stand up to the 'so what?' criticism that you've just found a random blip. It's unlikely that anyone would be churlish enough to criticise you in such tactless terms, but deep inside, you might well feel a smouldering unease, and a desire for some finding so stunningly unequivocal that it will strike would-be critics dumb with admiration. Honesty compels me to admit that some critics are so impervious to reason that there is little likelihood of anything making them change their brutish and barbarous ways, but others will at least have the decency to admit grudgingly that your logic and data are pure, which is a pretty good start. One way of achieving this is to demonstrate statistically what the odds are against your findings being a random blip, and one way of calculating these odds is to use inferential statistics.

Before you can use inferential statistics, though, you'll need to know something about measurement theory. We'll move on to measurement theory, and then return to descriptive statistics for some more detailed issues before proceeding to inferential statistics.

2

Measurement theory

Ratio values • Interval values • Ordinal measurements • Nominal categories

> *I could tell him anything that can even be attempted to be measured, except perhaps for the new mainyard, and I shall measure that with my tape before dinner.*
>
> (*Master and Commander*, p. 92)

Standard deviations are a Good Thing, and there are two types of them; averages are even more of a Good Thing, and there are no less than three types of them. Numbers are so much of a Good Thing that there are at least four different types of them (depending on your set of definitions). Why? This section discusses the moderately lengthy answer to this commendably brief question, and discusses some of the implications for you, your life and your research. Incidentally, if you are harbouring some dark suspicions about the parenthetic 'depending on your set of definitions' then your suspicions are justified: different authorities do indeed define the varieties of numbers in subtly different ways. Fortunately, they usually have the decency to explain these definitions early in their works, so if you're using a statistics textbook to decide which test to use, then you should find a section in it explaining how they are using the terms. The reason for these differences of opinion is not that statisticians don't know what they're doing; it's that different definitions are useful for different types of problem, and for different levels of simplification in introductory textbooks. The explanations used in this book are fairly standard, but you might find slightly different explanations elsewhere.

The previous chapter discussed limpets, and instances of dramatic prefiguration in Barbara Cartland. Both of these examples involve solid, respectable numbers that do all the things you might expect. In both cases, you'd not expect to see a value less than zero, such as 'minus five limpets' in a pool; in both cases, the gaps between the numbers are equally spaced, so that the gap between a value of 3 and a value of 5 is the same as the gap between a value of 23 and a value of 25. These are characteristics of measurement that look self-evident, and you might wonder why anyone would bother with any other sort. There are, however, fairly sensible reasons for having other types of measurement, and these tend to become apparent quite quickly when you are wrestling with the sordid realities of research. The following sections work through the types of numbers usually accepted within statistics, starting with the most familiar type of number.

Ratio values

Ratio values are what people usually think of as numbers – the gaps between numbers are equally spaced, and they have a zero (Figure 2.1).

Interval values

After the previous mentions of equally spaced gaps between numbers on ratio scales, it will come as little surprise to discover that there is a type of scale where the intervals are not equal: where the distance between a 2 and a 3, for instance, is not the same as the distance between a 5 and a 6 (see Figure 2.2). This, as you might imagine, plays hell with most varieties of arithmetic. Why should any-one be perverse enough to use such a thing? There are various sound reasons. Sometimes this was the best that anyone could manage at the time; sometimes, it's still the best that anyone can manage. The usual example is the Mohs scale in geology, which measures hardness of minerals, after a fashion. You have ten minerals in a little case, which you lug around the landscape with you; when you find a mineral that you don't recognise, you try scratching it with each of

Figure 2.1 A ratio scale

Figure 2.2   An interval scale

the ten minerals from your case in turn. If you know that it can be scratched by mineral number 5, but not mineral number 6, then its hardness is somewhere intermediate between 5 and 6, and you can turn to the 'minerals with hardness between 5 and 6' bit of your mineralogical handbook, having narrowed down the set of possibilities via this test. There's another way of measuring hardness on a more sensible scale, which involves a diamond, a micrometer and some bulky equipment; when this was invented, it produced the not unexpected finding that the gaps between the ten minerals on the Mohs scale were widely uneven. However, the Mohs minerals will fit in your jacket pocket, and the other kit won't, so the Mohs scale remains in routine use.

Another example more familiar to most readers involves questionnaires, which often ask you to give an answer on a five-point or seven-point scale. Sceptical purists occasionally ask unkind questions about whether these are on a ratio scale, as the perpetrators of the questionnaires usually claim, or are actually on an interval scale; they may go so far as to point to assorted psychological research suggesting that people answering such questionnaires do indeed use these as if they were interval scales. The perpetrators of the questionnaires tend to be understandably reluctant to accept this suggestion, since it would seriously limit the number of analyses they could perform on the resulting data. There are good arguments, when collecting data via questionnaires, for using visual analogue Likert-style scales, illustrated in Figure 2.3, since these work via the human visual system rather than its (somewhat dubious) numeric processing system. The scale is simply a horizontal line, usually 100 millimetres long, with a verbal label at each end; the respondent draws a vertical line through the scale at the appropriate point (e.g. about three quarters of the way along, if the answer is not 'completely' but is somewhere near). There's more about this later. There are strong, though not perfect, arguments for treating the resulting data as ratio values and therefore suitable for the most sophisticated forms of statistical analysis, but it's wiser not to push your luck with this if your supervisor disagrees.

Ordinal measurements

The next step down the path of 'least bad measurement type that we can manage' involves ordinal measurements. As the name might suggest, these

To what extent would you describe yourself as keen on reading?

not at all   completely

Figure 2.3   A visual analogue Likert-style scale

involve putting things in an order. This usually happens when you can't decently pretend that the data you're dealing with have even managed to scrabble up to the level of interval measurements. For example, if you're surveying people's attitudes to English-language authors, then respondents might generally agree that Shakespeare was a more prestigious author than Jeffrey Archer, with Iris Murdoch somewhere between the two, but might feel unable to place them on any sort of numeric scale. They could, however, place the three in a rank order, from most prestigious (Shakespeare, ranked 1) to least (Archer, ranked 3). A commercial example of this is the music charts, which simply rank the number of sales from the best seller downwards. In ranking systems of this sort, you only use whole numbers. For instance, if a new album comes straight into the charts between the current number three and the current number four, then you don't label it number 3.5; instead, you label it number four, and move all the others after it down one place. The situation is rather different with interval scales, where you can at a pinch use intermediate values; for instance, if you find a mineral which can be scratched by your number 3 mineral, but only just, then you might assign it a value a little above 3, such as 3.2.

Nominal categories

The last type of measurement is not, strictly speaking, a measurement at all; instead, it involves deciding which category to fit a specimen into. This doesn't involve any sort of scale, just a metaphorical label that you attach to the specimen. Some texts refer to these as nominal values, others refer to them as categorical information; I've used the term 'nominal categories' with a hint of overkill, to reduce the risk of misunderstanding. Common examples of nominal categories include religion, surnames and nationality, which don't form any sort of a scale, and where there aren't any intermediate values, just occasionally new categories that you'd missed previously. So, for example, the categories 'Jim' and 'Chris' don't form any sort of scale.

With names as examples, the situation is pretty clear. In the untidiness of the world, though, people sometimes use nominal terms as if they were on a scale. So, for instance, you might encounter statements such as: 'She's very French'. What this usually means is: 'She matches closely to my stereotype of a classic French person'. I have no malice towards nominal values, and a fair amount of my research has involved investigating them, but even their best friends have to admit that nominal values are a bit limited in terms of what you can do with them statistically.

With this information in mind, you might make an inward note to yourself to avoid dealing with nominal values if possible. A large number of students, however, throw this resolve away the instant they start designing a questionnaire. The classic example involves asking respondents to answer a question such as 'Are you an experienced Internet user?' with either a 'yes' or a 'no'. This means that the response is a nominal value, and this in turn means that the student would need to collect much more data than would have been the case if they had used some other type of measurement (such as 'How experienced an Internet user are you, on a scale where 1 represents "inexperienced" and 7 represents "very experienced"?'). Not, perhaps, the most elegant of phrasings, but questionnaire phrasings are seldom literary masterpieces. With that rant out of the way, this chapter draws to a close.

With measurement theory summarised, we'll pay a return visit to descriptive statistics. We'll begin by looking at some of the limitations which the different measurement types place on your analysis, and briefly discuss some classic sources of error, before moving on to more interesting things that descriptive statistics help you to do with your research.

3

Descriptive statistics

Means, rights, wrongs and debatable things • The bodegas of Glasgow: a tale of reliability and validity

> *It is questionable whether we can have complete confidence in Homer's figures, which, since he was a poet, were probably exaggerated.*
> (*History of the Peloponnesian War*, p. 41)

Life often features asymmetries which can, on occasion, be annoying. For instance, if you navigate five heavy, bulky bags of shopping through a dozen shops full of fragile items without brushing against a single piece of glassware, nobody will compliment you on your grace and skill. Knock over one miserable display of designer porcelain, however, and your previous successes will be ignominiously ignored. It's much the same with measurement theory and descriptive statistics. Nobody is likely to compliment you on your brilliant grasp of these topics when you get it right; make one miserable mistake, though, and unkind readers will pounce on it immediately, with no appreciation of your previously unblemished record. It may console you to know that your understanding of measurement theory can be positively useful later on, for things like reducing the amount of data that you need to collect for your chosen analysis. As regards simple descriptive statistics, though, your opportunities to shine are outweighed by the ways of making mistakes, so this chapter focuses on common errors that you might wish to avoid.

Means, rights, wrongs and debatable things

One particularly common error involves attempting to calculate means from the wrong types of measurement. The result will often be a commendably precise figure, but that figure will be meaningless, and, worse, will make you look like a raw beginner. There are various ways in which you might end up in this position. Sometimes the error is a technology-assisted error. A classic example is that you label some of your groups as 'group 1', 'group 2', etc. These are nominal values: you could replace these names with 'group A', 'group B', etc. without any change in meaning. If you have set up a spreadsheet to calculate means for your real, proper numbers, then you might inadvertently cut-and-paste a formula and end up with the formula helpfully calculating the alleged mean of the group names. It's easy enough to spot this in the cold light of day, but if it's three o'clock in the morning and your coursework deadline is a few hours away, you might be less perceptive.

With ordinal and interval measurements, the reasons for not trying to calculate means are more subtle. The problem with these is that the distances between each number are not equal. This means that you can't meaningfully add them together. If you're still not sure why this is the case, then imagine trying to measure distances with a ruler which is divided up as in Figure 3.1. If you're trying to add a distance of two units on this ruler to a distance of three units on this ruler, the answer may be five units, but the length covered by those five units will depend completely on which of the units you are using. The distance between unit 1 and unit 3, for instance, is a lot greater than the distance between 3 and 5.

Another favourite source of problems with means involves pooling data from several different data sets. Why is this problematic? A small example should make this clear. Suppose that you have been calculating the average weight of dogs brought in to your local vet, under the 'such other duties as shall from time to time be deemed reasonable by your boss' subsection which you didn't spot in your contract. A thousand dogs later, you have a mean figure of 24.6 kilos. A helpful friend then offers you some more data from another vet's dogs; this turns out to mean 'two data points, one apparently for an overweight Saint Bernard and the other allegedly for a Howondan elephant dog' with a mean figure of 75.4 kilos. So, how do you combine these data sets? The right thing to do is to add all the individual weights from both sets together, and then calculate the mean. This would give you a figure very slightly higher than the mean from your original very large group (just over

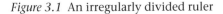

Figure 3.1 An irregularly divided ruler

24.7 kilos). The wrong thing to do is to add the two means together and try to calculate a mean between them; this would give you an answer of 50 kilos, since it has implicitly assumed that the two samples are equally numerous, which is not the case.

A similar issue relates to percentages. You can't take several percentage figures and try to calculate a mean between them; instead, you have to take the original figures from which the percentages were derived, and work from those, for the same reason as described above in relation to pooling data sets generally. So, for instance, if one sample of 1000 cats found that 46% of them preferred cat food A, and another sample of five cats found that 80% of them preferred cat food A, the right thing to do would be to work out a single percentage from the raw figures from both samples combined (giving a result of 46.17%). This is very different from what you would get by calculating the midpoint between 46 and 80, namely 63, which is much bigger and also sinful. On that improving note, we'll move on to a story of espionage and bars.

The bodegas of Glasgow: a tale of reliability and validity

During World War II, the German intelligence agencies encountered serious problems with their spies in Britain, who had a habit of being quickly detected by the British intelligence agencies. One spy, however, appeared to be a striking exception to this generalisation, and produced large quantities of information throughout much of the war. He described, for example, how morale in Glasgow had reached such a low point that there were men who would do anything for a litre of wine in the local bodega. Readers familiar with wartime Glasgow might be excused for feeling some suspicion about this account, and they would be right; when he wrote that report, the spy had not actually gone to Britain in the strict sense, and instead had generated his account in the more congenial setting of Portugal, using his imagination to fill in any bits for which he didn't have any real information, and using comfortably familiar concepts such as wine instead of beer, and bodegas instead of Glasgow bars.

Many written accounts of this episode make unkind comments about the credulity and bureaucratic mindlessness of the German spymasters, who assiduously processed these reports and passed them up the chain of command to feed into policy decisions. An interviewer in a documentary asked one of the spymasters about this. He claimed that he and his colleagues were well aware that the reports were works of fiction, but their options were (a) to edit out the more obviously fictitious bits, and produce voluminous analyses of the rest in triplicate, or (b) to admit that they didn't have a single spy working in Britain and had therefore totally failed in their task. Option (a) kept them in a nice office job with no heavy lifting; option (b) was likely to lead to bad experiences on the Eastern front. It wasn't a difficult decision. (Readers who do some homework will find that the spy in question was in fact a double agent working for the British; the full story is more complex than the brief account given above, and even more improbable.)

This story illustrates a point about statistics which is often overlooked in practice, namely the distinction between reliability and validity. Reliability comes in various forms, but the underlying point is that it involves getting a consistent set of findings. In the case of the Glaswegians doing anything for a litre of wine, for instance, there were consistent features across the spy's reports, such as low morale in Britain. In this sense, they were reliable. Validity, by contrast, involves whether the findings bear any relation to reality. The wine-loving Glaswegians clearly fell a bit short in this respect. It's horribly tempting to think that just because some findings are reliable in this statistical sense, then they must also be valid in the statistical sense – that if you keep finding the same thing consistently, then it must be true (especially if it supports your pet hunch, or if it keeps you in a nice safe office). Not so. If your initial data are essentially works of fiction on the part of your respondents, then any analysis you perform on the data, and any conclusions you draw, will also be works of fiction.

It's horribly easy to forget this point, or to give in to the siren voices telling you that you don't need to examine your initial assumptions too closely, especially if you have a nice, shiny statistical test that you want to play with for the first time, or a metaphorical warehouse full of untouched data. You don't want to find out that the data can't be trusted, and that you've wasted large amounts of time collecting the equivalent of wine lists for Glasgow pubs in World War II.

A related source of confusion for many researchers is that the words 'reliable' and 'valid' are used with quite different meanings by different groups of people. In ordinary English, for example, 'reliable' is often used to mean 'trustworthy'. For this reason, many researchers use technical phrases to reduce the risk of misunderstanding. For example, the phrase 'test-retest reliability' means 'the extent to which you get the same answer when you apply the same test to someone on more than one occasion'; the phrase 'inter-rater reliability' means 'the extent to which two or more different individuals will independently give the same rating to a given item on the specified rating system'. Similarly, 'external validity' means 'the extent to which these findings correspond to reality' (setting aside temporarily the philosophical debate about the nature of reality). A classic example used by world-weary lecturers is that descriptions of Father Christmas have high reliability, since the overwhelming majority of respondents describe him in almost identical terms, but low external validity, because Father Christmas does not exist. I will resist the temptation to comment on this.

If you use technical phrases such as those just described, then your meaning is unambiguous, and everyone can get on with life. It's important, however, to remember that different disciplines use different phrases, so you should find out what the usual phrasing is in your discipline, and use that. Fortunately, there's pretty general agreement between disciplines about what the concepts are, even if there are some differences about what they're called.

That's probably enough description of sin for one chapter, so we'll move on to the next, which is about ways of viewing and presenting your data.

4

Patterns in data and presentation of data

A mud pit to avoid: the inappropriate graph • Patterns of data

> *He saw and appreciated all he was meant to see. He was blind to the things he was not meant to see.*
>
> (*Master and Commander*, p. 24)

In an ideal world, virtue would always be rewarded, sin would always be punished, and you would never have to do group work. The reality, alas, is somewhat different. This chapter rights the balance at least a little by using group work as an example, and by looking at sins likely to be committed by your fellow group workers.

There are cheerful references to representations like pie charts in the early part of this chapter, on the assumption that most readers will have enough idea of what these are to make sense of the text without slowing it down for explanations at this point; there is then more detail about the nature and limitations of each representation later in the chapter. As usual with stats, there are many relevant concepts; as usual, I've skimmed swiftly through them because of word-count limitations. On, then, to your imaginary group.

Imagine that you've been asked to do a survey about use of the Internet, with particular reference to the role of Internet experience as a variable. With depressing predictability, a pushy male has appointed himself group leader; the depressingly predictable next step is that the least assertive woman in the group is appointed as scribe, but we'll assume that your group has virtuously allocated this role by drawing straws. The bad news is that you get the short straw; the good news is that you're excused from data collection in consequence. The pushy male group leader then decrees that everyone will collect their data simultaneously to save time, and that the group will put all their data together to make one big data set. The following week, you meet to compare results, starting with your esteemed leader.

He proudly displays the pie chart shown in Figure 4.1, where the size of each piece of pie corresponds to the proportion of respondents fitting into that category. It looks like a pretty clear difference, until you ask about the sample sizes, and you discover that the sample consists of six experienced and four inexperienced Internet users. This is not an impressively large sample on which to base any conclusions, but the smallness of the sample was obscured by the use of a pie chart without any mention of the *n*.

Taking a further step into the heart of darkness, another group member asks how he has operationalised his metrics, namely what he means by 'experienced' and 'inexperienced'. It turns out that he hasn't specified this to his respondents, and has allowed them to use whatever definitions they wanted, without asking them what those definitions were. Not a good start.

The next group member has at least thought about this issue, and has used the definition of 'using the Internet on four or more days per week' – in other words, using it on more days than they do not use it. He presents the chart shown in Figure 4.2 for his results from a sample of ten younger people and ten older people. This is a **bar chart**, as opposed to a **histogram**: on a bar chart, you can have the bars in any order you want along the horizontal axis, whereas in a histogram, there's some form of scale along the horizontal axis as well as the vertical axis, so the order of the bars is predetermined.

The scale line going up the vertical axis shows the number of respondents in each group, which makes it clear how small the distance is between them. On the subject of small distances, the logistical problem of fitting labels onto the groups in a bar chart is also fairly clear in this example, and is one reason why so much published research involves short, cryptic names for the groups, such as 'group A' rather than something more lyrical. (Yes, you can persuade the software to write the group names vertically, which is fine if you don't mind

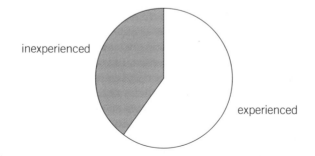

Figure 4.1 A sinful pie chart without numbers

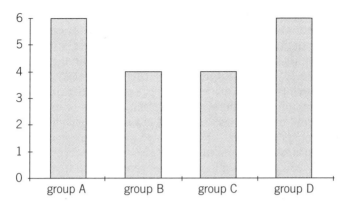

Group A: younger respondents, experienced in Internet use
Group B: younger respondents, not experienced in Internet use
Group C: older respondents, experienced in Internet use
Group D: older respondents, not experienced in Internet use

Figure 4.2 Bar chart of Internet use among younger and older people

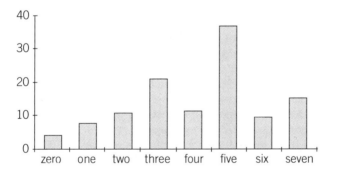

Figure 4.3 Number of days per week on which respondents use the Internet

annoying any readers who object to having to having the text on your bar
chart going in two directions simultaneously.)

You can do a certain amount with a result such as '46% of my older respondents considered themselves experts on the Internet', but it's unlikely that
this will either set the world on fire or give enough raw material for an impressive group mark. The situation improves when the next group member
presents her results. She has asked the respondents to say on how on many
days per week they use the Internet. This changes the data from simple nominal values of 'expert' and 'non-expert' into a set of ratio values on a scale.
If you plot the results on a histogram, you might get the results shown in
Figure 4.3.

This histogram raises various questions that would not be raised by the simple experienced/inexperienced grouping of respondents. For instance, there's a bimodal distribution, with the most common response involving Internet use five days a week, followed by the next most common being Internet use three days a week. What might this mean? There are various possible explanations; one is that the 'five days per week' response is from people who use the Internet at work, but not at home, with the 'three days per week' coming from people who don't use the Internet at work, but who use it in their leisure time on Friday evenings and at weekends; the next most common response, 'seven days per week', would be consistent with respondents using the Internet for work during the week, and for leisure at weekends. These are just guesses, but they're plausible guesses, and could be investigated via a follow-up study.

Another thing that the histogram shows is what could have gone wrong with the definition of expertise about the Internet as 'using the Internet on four days per week or more'. That definition was semi-arbitrary; if it had been changed to 'more than one day per week', on the grounds that this implied regular use, then the vast majority of respondents would be classed as 'expert'. If it had been changed to 'seven days per week' to catch the daily users, then the definition would have excluded the high proportion of respondents who were probably using the Internet every working day, but not at weekends.

Questions and speculations such as these can lead to new studies, and to changes in how you gather your evidence. By this point, your group might be wondering whether it would have been better to ask more detailed questions about when the respondents use the Internet, and for what purpose. To your delight, the next group member turns out to have done just that, and more. He asked respondents to give their age, and to say how many hours per week they spent using the Internet for leisure activities. People can be reticent about giving their exact age, and a common way round this problem is to ask them to say which age band they fall into, with options such as 21–30 years old, 31–40 and so on. If you do this, a bar chart might show something along the lines of Figure 4.4 for each age band.

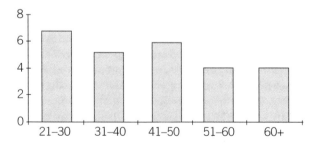

Figure 4.4 Time per week spent using the Internet for leisure (mean figure, in hours)

This shows a high value for the youngest of the age bands, followed by a dip for the respondents in the 31–40 band, and then a rise for the respondents aged 41–50, after which the figures drop off. Again, the results suggest further possible questions. For instance, why is there a dip for the second age band, and then a rise again? One possible explanation is that some respondents in that age band might be parents of young children, and therefore have less leisure time, lowering the figure from what it would otherwise have been. This, though, is just a guess. If you happened to have data for respondents' family circumstances, then you could analyse respondents with young children separately from the rest, to see whether that is a plausible reason for the dip. If you didn't happen to have that data, then you'd either need to accept that this explanation was just a guess, or do some more work.

This makes it clear that there's an overall downwards trend. You might wonder, however, whether this trend is a completely misleading by-product from some hideously aberrant data lurking within the innocuous-looking phrase 'mean figure'. Might, for instance, the figures for 21–30-year-olds be seriously skewed by a few individuals who spent every spare moment obsessively surfing the Net, while the rest got on with improving hobbies unrelated to computers? It's possible. One way of finding out would be to look at the standard deviations and extreme values. It's a good way, but not as visually striking as a **scattergram**, illustrated in Figure 4.5. If you were able to obtain the exact age of each respondent, which isn't beyond the realm of possibilities, and you plotted the age of each individual respondent against how long that

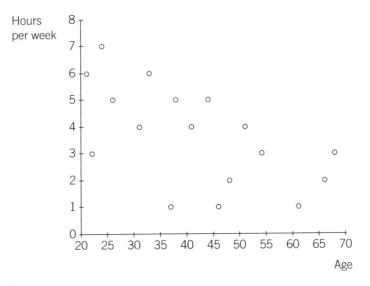

Figure 4.5 Scattergram of age plotted against hours per week spent using the Internet for leisure

respondent spent using the Internet for leisure, then you might get something like this.

This shows that there is an overall negative **correlation** – i.e. as age increases, leisure use of the Internet decreases – but there are quite a few exceptions to this general trend. Some of these exceptions might be because of random variations; some might be because there are sub-groups of respondents who differ in some way, such as lifestyle or income. How can you tell which is the case? You can use inferential statistics to assess the likelihood of the variation being due to random chance, as described in the chapters on inferential statistics; you can do a further study to gather more information; you can also make some reasonable inferences (or at least, plausible guesses) by eyeballing the data, i.e. inspecting the data by eye, which is the topic of the final part of this chapter.

It would be tempting at this point to use the last couple of days before the hand-in date to rush out and do a proper systematic survey where all of you used the same, sensible phrasings on your subject instruction sheets and data collection sheets. What would happen?

One likely outcome is that the new data would gradually converge on a fairly stable set of results. For example, the mean figure for weekly Internet use among respondents aged 30–39 might be 4.1 hours for the first ten respondents; after twenty respondents, the mean figure for the twenty respondents might rise to 4.2 hours. The next batches of data added to the total sample might produce revised figures of 4.13, 4.19 and 4.17 hours, respectively. By this stage, you might be suspecting that the figure is now going to stay stubbornly somewhere between 4.1 and 4.2 hours no matter how much the sample size is increased. That suspicion is probably right; unless you change the type of people you're sampling, or the questions you're asking them, it's a pretty good bet that adding more data won't change the overall picture. This is, in fact, a useful way of answering the age-old question: 'How big a sample do I need?' Once the results have stabilised in this way (which they tend to do sooner than novices expect) then there's not much point in wasting resources gathering more data.

This leads on to the issue of whether a finding is worth getting in the first place. There's a conceptual difference between the **statistical significance** of an effect and its **power**. The statistical significance is the likelihood that a particular difference is due to nothing more than simple coincidence. For instance, you might test a new teaching method, find that students taught with this method perform better than students taught with the old method, and find that statistically there's only one chance in a thousand that the difference is due to the new-method students all coincidentally just happening to perform better than usual in the test. That's the level of statistical significance. However, just because an effect has a high level of statistical significance, that doesn't mean that the effect does very much. Suppose you're comparing two new teaching methods. Both produce results with a significance level of one chance in a thousand, but the first method produces a mean improvement of only 1% in test scores, whereas the second method produces a mean improvement of 23%. The second method clearly has a much more powerful effect than the second, even though it's at the same level of statistical significance. There are ways of calculating how big a sample you'd need if you wanted to test for a given power of effect – for instance, 'How many children would I need to use this teaching method on before I could tell whether or not it was (say) 10% better than the old method at a statistically significant level?'. It's a sensible thing to do if you're doing a real, solid professional study that will affect people's lives – if so, you should talk to a statistician before firming up the study plans.

A related note which was mentioned earlier is that it's a good thing to tell the reader the extreme values, mean, etc. for your data. It's also possible to show this information in a diagram. One widely used method is to draw what are known as **error bars** around each point on a scattergram; another is to draw what are known as **box plots**. Both these methods can be handy when each point in your scattergram shows a mean value for a group of data, rather than a single value for a single specimen. For example, you might be plotting the attention span of small boys at different ages, with one group aged 2 and another group aged 4. Figure 4.6 shows results for two groups of subjects, with the black circles showing the means for the two groups. The group on the left has a lower mean value than the group on the right. The line stuck through the middle of each circle shows the standard deviation for each group, with the top end of the line showing the value for one standard deviation above the mean, and the bottom end of the line showing the value for one standard deviation below it. The first group has a smaller standard deviation than the second group. Box plots are based on a similar concept, but with a rectangle in

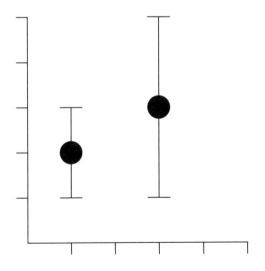

Figure 4.6 Error bars

the middle rather than a circle, and with dots showing the extreme values for the data; the rectangle in the middle contains yet more information about medians and various other things which space and balance prevent me from describing in lyrical detail.

Anyway, around this point you might be wondering what happened to the other traditional group member who didn't put in any work and who didn't even show up for the group meetings. The answer, since this is a brief chunk of ideal world, is that the lecturer found out about their slacking and ensured that Something Bad happened to them. Something Very Bad. Something So Bad that they returned to the group looking terrified and repentant, and diligently did the whole of the big data collection exercise in an exemplary fashion as penance, bringing back a beautiful data set in plenty of time for the write-up, so you all get a distinction. We'll leave the group work at this point, with sinners rectified, and with virtue rewarded. Next, we'll visit a couple of classic mud pits into which beginners sometimes fall.

A mud pit to avoid: the inappropriate graph

One classic mud pit involves prettily coloured figures – pie charts are a particular favourite. These typically look very striking on the monitor screen; they don't look so striking if you run them through a monochrome photocopier or printer and end up with group A depicted in a fetching shade of light grey, and group B depicted in an equally fetching and practically identical shade of light grey. It's horribly easy to make this mistake when under pressure from a deadline. It's also worth considering that quite a lot of people are colour blind to various degrees, so using colour alone as a differentiator in your diagrams is not the greatest of ideas.

A more subtle common error among beginners is the inappropriate graph. To illustrate the nature of the error, Figure 4.7 shows an example of a proper, respectable line graph, showing managers' ratings on your newly developed scale for measuring idealism. It shows a classic straight line, with the 20-year-old managers scoring quite high for idealism, but the 30-year-olds scoring less high, and the 40-year-olds scoring lower still. Let's now suppose that you wanted to know how 25-year-old managers would score: how could you find out? One way would be to test a batch of them, but looking at Figure 4.7, it's a pretty fair bet that their scores would be exactly midway between the scores of the 20-year-olds and the scores of the 30-year-olds. Similarly, if you wanted to predict the scores of 35-year-olds, you could just look at the graph line midway between the 30-year-olds and the 40-year-olds.

Suppose now that we have the bar chart in Figure 4.8, showing idealism ratings among individual managers. With the line graph, the point midway between '20-year-old' and '30-year-old' represented '25-year-old'. What does

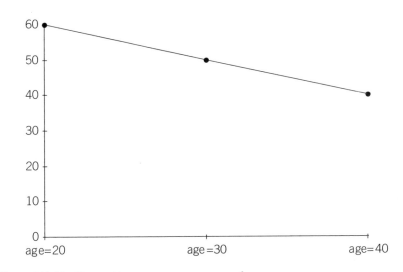

Figure 4.7 Idealism ratings among managers, by age

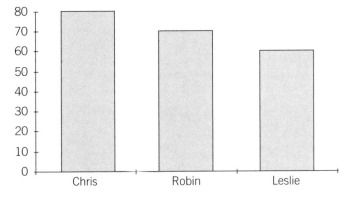

Figure 4.8 Idealism among individual managers

the point midway between 'Chris' and 'Robin' mean on the bar chart above? It means nothing: the three names don't form a scale, and the order they're in is pretty much arbitrary, so you could as easily have Leslie in the middle instead of Robin. Line graphs can be used to allow you to work out what intermediate values are likely to be, and they depend on having a scale along your horizontal axis. If your horizontal axis can't show a scale, then you can't use a line graph. If your horizontal axis shows nominal values (which by definition can't form a scale), such as names of people, faiths, nationalities, species or preferred brand of car, then you can't use a line graph, and you have to use a different representation – bar charts are usually the best bet.

At one level, the reader can usually tell pretty easily what sort of thing you're showing on your horizontal axis, so there's not a huge risk that you'll mislead them. At another level, though, Cynical Readers (such as lecturers marking your work) will view an inappropriate line graph as a sign that you've failed to grasp the distinction between numbers and names, which is a pretty basic concept in statistics, and will mark you down for that shortcoming; they'll also wonder whether you might have made any other, more subtle, errors which might give them more of a challenge, and more opportunity to write incisive comments in red pen on your work.

On that cheering note, we'll move on to look at some of the patterns that you might find in your data, and to talk about what these patterns can tell you.

Patterns of data

When you look at data for a while, you start seeing patterns. Sometimes these patterns are real; sometimes they're the by-product of the human visual system, which is so keen on finding patterns that it can see the face of Elvis in a blemish on a taco. How can you tell which is the case? Sometimes you can't; sometimes you can use inferential statistics, but that's another subject, and will be covered later (in Chapter 7).

A useful first stab is to plot your data in a scattergram (described in more detail below); you can then see how it compares to the various patterns and shapes which are also described below. We'll start with lines in graphs because they should be easier to grasp.

For clarity, the illustrations below sometimes have numbers missing on the horizontal axis, but you should be aware that this is normally a bad habit, and one not to be indulged outside textbooks using imaginary data, otherwise Cynical Readers might suspect that you are trying to distort your data.

Patterns you might find in graphs

One classic pattern you might find in graphs is the straight line: as one variable gets bigger, another gets consistently bigger or consistently smaller. If they're both getting bigger (or both getting smaller) then it's known as a **positive correlation**; if one gets bigger while the other gets smaller, then it's known as a **negative correlation**. If you plot children's ages against their weight, for instance, then there's a positive correlation until they stop growing in their late teens. A perfect positive correlation looks something like Figure 4.9. As one of these variables increases, the other increases at the same rate. A perfect negative correlation is very similar, except that it slopes in the opposite direction (Figure 4.10). In this example, as one variable gets larger, the other gets smaller at the same rate.

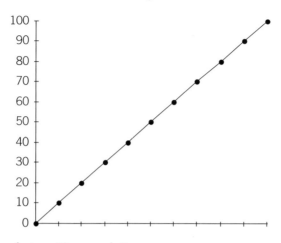

Figure 4.9 A perfect positive correlation

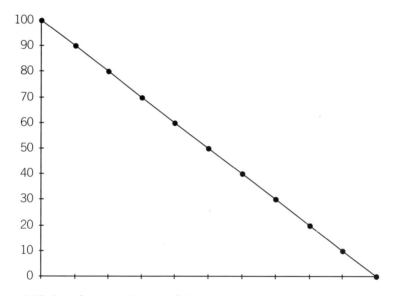

Figure 4.10 A perfect negative correlation

It's rare to get such straight-line correlations in real data, but not impossible: I have vivid memories of the time when a colleague doing some psychological research rushed into the coffee room and showed everyone a graph where his data formed a line so straight that, even with his sharpest pencil, the line passed neatly through the middle of each data point on the line (this was in the days of pencils and graph paper, which might say something about the rarity of such events). More often, the data wobble about a bit, and form a line which is fairly but not utterly straight. How much wobbling would still count as a correlation, and how much would constitute random variation with no trace of a correlation? That's a question that can be handled by use of inferential statistics, and it's answered it in the chapters on inferential statistics (Chapter 7) and correlations (Chapter 9). For now, though, we'll stay on the topic of eyeballing the data from your descriptive stats.

Still on the subject of data forming discernible lines, it's possible to find lines which are obvious in the data, but which are a shape other than straight (**nonlinear**, to use the technical term). Some classic patterns are as follows.

In Figure 4.11, the values drop off quite steeply at first, but then drop off more slowly after that. You find results like this, for instance, if you test people's memory for a list of items: their memory is pretty good for the first day, then drops off steeply over the next few days, and levels off after that. Quite a lot of things follow this pattern; it can look pretty alarming if the figures are for some social trend that looks set to crash into a disastrous zero in the near future, but usually the trend levels off at the last moment. (Usually, but not always: such situations are nerve-racking precisely because you can't be sure what the trend will do.) This principle can also work the other way – for instance, you might be hoping fervently that your new approach will cause tuberculosis rates to drop to zero, but there's that uneasy feeling that the rates might not quite get there, because of a last-minute levelling off.

You can also get curves which go in the other direction, increasing more and more steeply as in Figure 4.12. Just as the early stages of a descending curve bear a marked resemblance to the early stages of a straight line heading towards zero, so the later stages of an ascending curve might look as if they'll

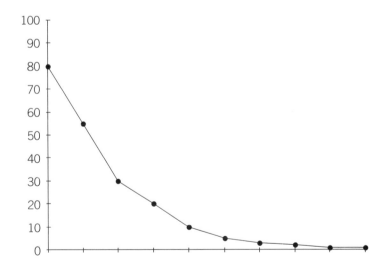

Figure 4.11 A descending curve

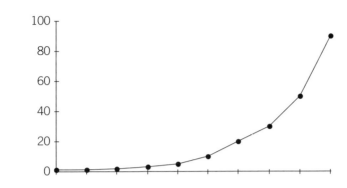

Figure 4.12 An increasing curve

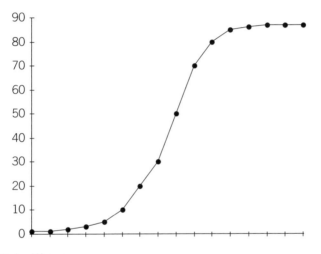

Figure 4.13 An 'S' curve

continue increasing steeply forever. Perpetrators of pyramid selling schemes, for instance, are keen to encourage this sort of belief.

More often, though, the curve does something different, and forms what is known as an 'S' curve (Figure 4.13). A fairly common pattern is that something starts off slowly, speeds up dramatically for a while, and then steadies down again.This is a typical pattern for sales of a new product, such as mobile phones: there's a slow early phase, then a period of rapid sales, and then things level off when the market is saturated.

Bad People sometimes helpfully tweak graphs like this to illustrate their message more clearly. Suppose, for instance, that you want to convince investors that this is a very fast-growing market, and that they should buy shares in your product now, while they have a chance to make huge profits on the rapidly rising market. You might present the graph with the vertical axis helped along a bit by some stretching, as in Figure 4.14.

If, on the other hand, you want to convince voters that an apparently scary trend is nothing to worry about, and that you should be re-elected to keep things under control, then you might clarify this by tweaking the vertical axis in the other direction, and possibly stretching the horizontal axis while you're about it, as in Figure 4.15. A nice, flat curve like this looks much more soothing to persons of a nervous disposition.

There are assorted other ways of creatively presenting graphs, such as omitting bits of them; this is why Cynical Readers tend to be purists, and like to see clear, unambiguous labels on both the horizontal and vertical axis. They might also like to know why you started your graph with the figure for 2002, rather than, say, 2001 or 2003 – they might be wondering, for instance, whether you chose that particular year as a starting point because it produced a curve on your graph which suited your personal agenda. If you're starting to wonder miserably whether this means that everything is arbitrary, then be reassured: statistics is not a quagmire of cynical relativism, for reasons that we'll cover in

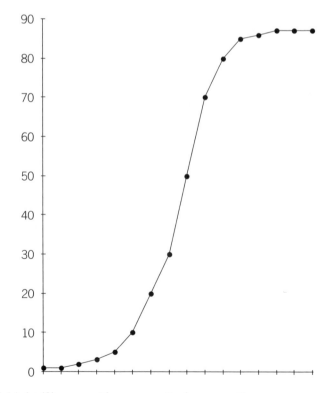

Figure 4.14 An 'S' curve with some vertical exaggeration

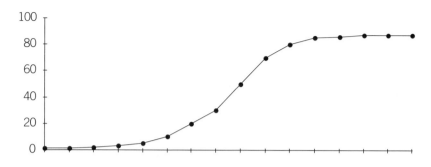

Figure 4.15 An 'S' curve with some vertical compression and horizontal stretching

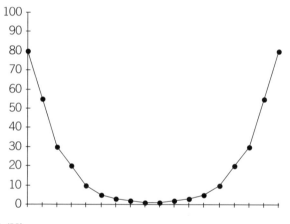

Figure 4.16 A 'U' curve

more detail in a later chapter. For the moment, though, we'll return to patterns in data, in the form of the 'U' curve, which will also feature again in a later chapter, when we deal with correlations.

In a 'U' curve (Figure 4.16), the value drops to a low point, then rises to a high point again. This is a pattern which can show up when you're representing something seasonal, such as the number of cold-weather migratory birds showing up at a wildlife sanctuary, or something involving a longer time scale, such as number of visits to the doctor per from birth till old age. You can also get the same pattern the other way up, so it forms a hump in the middle with low points at each end, in an inverted 'U' curve. A classic thing to beware with Us and inverted Us is attempting to calculate inappropriate correlations for the data in them – what can happen is that you get a spurious result claiming that there's no correlation, because the positive correlation from the first half of the data is cancelled out by a matching negative correlation from the second half of the data.

Patterns you might find in scattergrams

Scattergrams can be useful for showing patterns of distribution involving groups. A scattergram is a diagram showing a horizontal axis with a scale on it, and a vertical axis with a scale on it; each one of your bits of data is then shown at the appropriate point on the diagram. (For instance, in the scattergram in Figure 4.17 there's a data point about eight units along and five units up from the bottom left corner of the diagram.) Scattergrams are known by various names, including 'scatter plot' and 'scatter diagram'; 'scattergram' sounds consistent with 'histogram' and 'diagram', so it's widely used even if pedants don't always approve.

In Figure 4.17, there's a positive correlation between the two variables. It's not a perfect straight-line correlation – there's some variability, but the overall trend is clearly a positive correlation. The two groups in this scattergram both show the same overall pattern of correlation, but group A has consistently lower values than group B, and the two groups don't overlap. You might get this sort of pattern if you plotted height against weight for adult dogs from a small and a large breed of dog (assuming the two breeds were approximately the same shape).

Groups on scattergrams often overlap, as in the example in Figure 4.18, where groups A and B overlap. Group B has a broad range of values; group

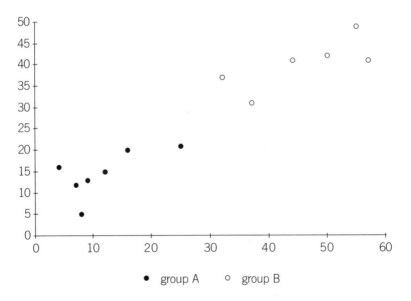

Figure 4.17 A scattergram of two separate groups

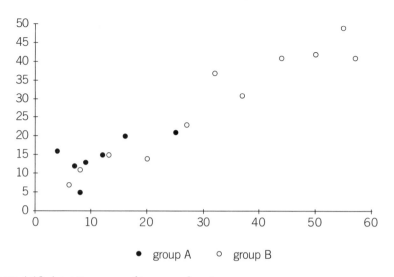

Figure 4.18 A scattergram of two overlapping groups

A has a comparatively small range of values. You might find a result like this if you plotted height against weight for dogs of different ages from two breeds; the younger pups of the two breeds would overlap in size, but the older pups and the adults of the bigger breed would grow beyond the maximum size of the smaller breed.

Scattergrams can also show that your data consist of more or less random noise, as in Figure 4.19. If there is a pattern in this example, then it's not immediately visible. The values for both groups are scattered across the diagram, with no obvious trend. There are few very low values for group A, but given the wide variation across group A, this might be purely a chance finding.

Patterns you might find in bar charts

Bar charts can also tell you many interesting things about your data. We'll begin with a couple of those things, both of which might suggest that you need to rethink your research design, namely ***floor*** and ***ceiling*** effects.

The scores for all the groups in Figure 4.20 are very near to zero. This implies that a lot of the scores from individual respondents were actually zero. This in turn implies that the method being used to get these scores (in this case the Base Jumping Aptitude Test) is not sensitive enough to measure anything other than a very large result. If the data are consistently low like this, it's known as a 'floor effect' because most of the scores are at ground level. In some situations, low scores of this sort may be the whole point – for instance, you might be displaying survival rates from a particularly unpleasant disease, and focusing on how lethal it is. In other situations, low scores might simply mean that the measuring method is too crude to pick up anything other than the very largest effects.

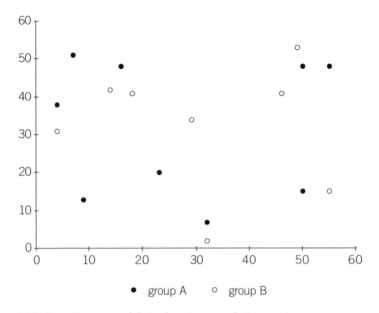

Figure 4.19 A scattergram of data showing no obvious pattern

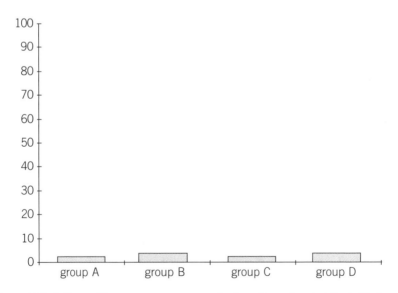

Figure 4.20 A floor effect: mean scores on the Base Jumping Aptitude Test

You may wonder whether there's a converse effect, and there is: it's known as the 'ceiling effect', and it tends to happen when you're using a measuring instrument which stops too low – the equivalent of measuring high-jumping ability among schoolchildren when the upper limit of your high jump is 45 centimetres. It looks something like the bar chart in Figure 4.21. This hypothetical example shows student performance on the school's own in-house test, as featured in advertising material. The fact that the mean scores are so near to 100% suggests that a lot of the individual scores were actually 100%, suggesting that the test was very easy.

Floor and ceiling effects are pretty well known. A more interesting example of something you can detect via bar charts is outliers, as in Figure 4.22. (Outliers are also usually obvious in scattergrams, as isolated dots far from the others.) The hypothetical results in this example show the number of respondents who scored within the stated range in a test – so, for instance, twelve were in the 1–25 range and twenty-eight were in the 26–50 range. The largest single group of respondents, however, was the group of respondents who scored 0 in the test. You'd expect some respondents to score 0 if you tested a lot of them, but not this high a proportion – you'd expect it to be less than the number who scored between 1 and 25. An outlier of this size suggests that there was something odd going on, such as a large number of respondents completely misunderstanding the instructions in the test. Improbable? If you read Stephen Jay Gould's book *The Mismeasure of Man*, you'll find examples of just this sort from real, early intelligence testing. Large numbers of zero scores are often an indicator that there's something wrong in the data collection.

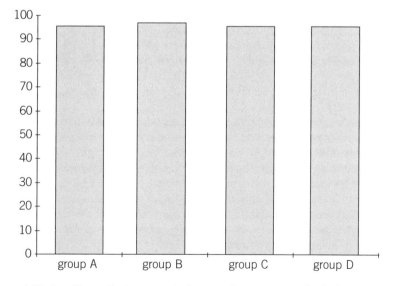

Figure 4.21 A ceiling effect: mean student performance on the in-house test

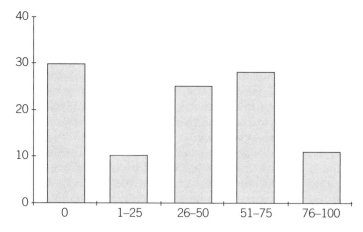

Figure 4.22 Anomalous outliers in test scores

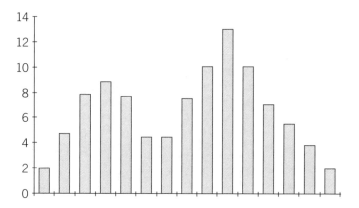

Figure 4.23 A bimodal distribution

Another indicator worth watching for when you're coding data is when the number of responses that you categorise under 'other' or 'miscellaneous' is larger than the number of responses that occur in one of your non-miscellaneous categories. If this happens, it suggests that you need to rethink the categories that you're using in your coding.

In the discussion of scattergrams earlier, there was a reference to representing groups in your data. That's fine if you know in advance what your groups will be, but how can you tell whether there are separate groups within your data which you hadn't noticed, and which you'd inadvertently lumped together? This is something for which histograms can be useful, as in the example in Figure 4.23. This histogram shows data with two clear and quite separate modes, one at 9 and one at 13. A distribution with two modes is

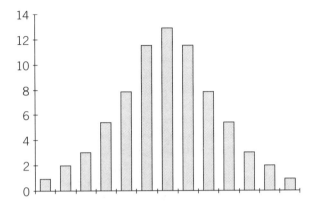

Figure 4.24 A normal distribution

known as a **bimodal distribution**, and its presence suggests that you might have two separate groups within this batch of data.

Finally, as is customary in statistics books, there is another pattern which frequently appears on histograms. It is known as the **normal distribution** or the **Gaussian distribution**. You'll encounter it repeatedly in the remainder of this book. As the choice of names might suggest, it's a distribution which statisticians have pondered about at some length, though you'll probably prefer to be spared the details of its relationship to concepts such as the standard normal distribution and the Poisson distribution in an introductory book such as this one. We'll use the name 'normal distribution' from now on. It looks something like Figure 4.24.

Right, that's it for graphs, scattergrams and suchlike for the time being. You might by this stage be wondering about some of the cheerful implicit assumptions involved in creating some of these representations; questions such as 'What if things don't fit neatly into categories?' might be flitting across your mind. If you're thinking such thoughts, then you're right to do so; these and related questions will be the topic of the next chapter.

5

'None of the above': the role of knowledge representation

On categorisation and pigeon-holes • Patterns • Graphs and nets • Things to watch out for

This is a brig, sir; though we call her a sloop.

(*Master and Commander*, p. 94)

Cookery books can be sadly uninspired at times, as I once discovered when seeking ideas about how to cook some kohlrabi: being advised to 'treat it as a turnip' is not terribly helpful to anyone with either a vivid imagination or an acquaintance with the literature on aberrant human behaviour. Many statistics books give much the same impression: you get the feeling that unless you're doing formal experiments on rats, humans or plants, then you shouldn't really consider yourself a proper researcher. In fairness to writers of statistics books, much of this impression is misleading; many of the relevant issues fall outside the realm of statistics in the strict sense. In an ideal world, these issues would be picked up neatly by another discipline, such as research design, but in practice the long-suffering issues tend to be viewed as something similar to a patch of bare moorland on the border between two provinces, just about worth planting a flag on, but not worth a proper survey, or a page to itself in the atlas. This is an unfortunate state of affairs, which is addressed in this chapter. It's tempting to extend the analogy by comparing the border territory to an area full of previously unsuspected riches, like Alaska's gold and oil, but I'll resist that opportunity, and instead will say a few words about ways of describing your field in a manner that lets you ask and answer more interesting questions than might otherwise be the case.

This chapter is loosely based on the literature on knowledge representation, which is a well-established field in its own right within artificial intelligence, to which I have added various bits from other areas. For the usual reasons, I've not gone into detail about most of the concepts below, but you should be able to track them down pretty easily, since they're fairly standard.

It's unlikely that you'll meet the concepts below in a stats exam, but they can be useful as a way of avoiding some classic problems in your research design. If you're going on to do original research of your own (e.g. as a PhD student) then you might find some of these concepts useful in a more positive sense, as giving ideas about new ways of tackling problems in your field. If you're an over-stretched student trying to struggle through the compulsory stats module, on the other hand, then you can skip this chapter completely if you want to, without needing to fear bad things happening later on. The concept names are in **bold** but not in italics, as a reminder that they're technical terms mostly from outside statistics; an online search using these terms as keywords should find plenty of further material about them.

On categorisation and pigeon-holes

A lot of research involves putting things into metaphorical pigeon-holes. This may take the form of a questionnaire asking you to describe yourself as married, single or divorced; it may take the form of the coding categories that you use for content analysis of a text; it may take the form of assigning a flint artefact to a particular culture such as the Solutrean, or a work of art to a school such as art nouveau. As anyone who's been on the receiving end of this experience will probably testify, trying to fit things into pigeon-holes can be a very unsatisfactory experience.

Suppose, for instance, that you're asked what your surname is. A lot of married women use two surnames, namely their married name and their maiden name, for different purposes; if you're only allowed to answer with one of these names, then there are obvious potential problems. Even apparently unambiguous questions can lead into strange territory. For instance, a survey some years ago allegedly found that 0.5% of people in the UK did not know whether or not they owned a motor bike. This sounds pretty unlikely, given the utter tangibility of a motor bike, but a moment's reflection produces some perfectly sensible reasons for not knowing whether or not you own one. Suppose, for instance, that you are buying one on hire purchase; does that count as 'owning'? What if you have bought one jointly with your mate; does that count? What if you've ordered one, but it hasn't arrived yet?

If such a simple question can lead to problems, then the prospects for more complex questions might look depressing. One traditional response is to pretend there isn't a problem and then to press on regardless; another is to do the best you can, make a few remarks about insoluble problems in the write-up, and to press on regardless; a third is to turn to nihilism and claim that everything is relative. Comparatively few people respond by wondering whether there's a literature about categorisation problems of this sort, and even fewer go on to find that such a literature exists, let alone make use of it. That's unfortunate, because (a) that literature provides a lot of useful methodological and conceptual tools which might help your research, and (b) just mentioning it in your references should be good for a brownie point or two, even if you don't actually use it.

There are various ways of handling categories. One is to treat them like fences: there's a dividing line, and everything is either on one side of it or on the other. In linguistics, for instance, there's the concept of **minimal pairs**: words which only differ by one sound, such as 'red' and 'led' in English, where the distinction between 'r' and 'l' is the fence. Within the fence, there's commendable equality: one 'r' is as good as another 'r'. That all sounds terribly sensible, until you realise that there's a completely opposite, but equally sensible approach, in which you treat categories as being a bit like feudal kingdoms. In this approach, each category has a set of core members, a bit like the central provinces, with the allegiance of provinces weakening as you get further from the capital, until finally you reach debatable frontier territory where there's no agreement about who a particular chunk of territory belongs to. In medicine, for instance, some syndromes are a bit like this: you get some cases which show all the symptoms and clearly belong to that syndrome, other cases which show most of the symptoms and probably belong, and yet other cases which show a few symptoms of one syndrome but also show a few symptoms of another.

There are various ways of systematising these concepts, which can help you to ask more interesting research questions. **Prototype theory**, in psychology, deals with the 'feudal kingdoms' cases, and researchers in this tradition have done a fair amount of research into how people prefer to categorise things. If you're more mathematically inclined, you can use **fuzzy logic**, which allows you to put a number on how strongly something belongs to a category. The numbers involved are usually decimals between 0 and 1, for historical reasons. For instance, you might view a Porsche as belonging strongly to the category 'sports car', with a value of 0.9, whereas a Ford Escort would belong less strongly, with a value of 0.5, and a Reliant Robin might only belong weakly, with a value of 0.1. If that sounds a bit intimidating, one simple way of turning this to advantage is to team up with a tame mathematician and produce some joint work, where you handle your area and the mathematician does the fuzzy logic: the results should be interesting whatever you find.

Patterns

Patterns, as Evingolis remarked, tend to fall within a frame; there are regularities in behaviour. Again, there are formalisms which describe this in a way that can be combined with statistics, and which allow you to ask more interesting questions. Approaches such as **story grammars** and **script theory** describe the underlying regularities beneath the surface details in actions. For example, Propp studied the underlying regularities in Russian folk tales, and found recurrent patterns, such as the hero being banished while young. At a more mundane level, something like eating in a restaurant has the regular script of eating appetisers, then first course and main course followed by dessert and coffee, and so on. Examples of this sort are so familiar that we tend not to notice them until we encounter a different pattern, such as a first encounter with a Chinese restaurant. If you're statistically inclined, you can do things like measure the **minimum edit distance** between two of these patterns, which sounds pretty impressive, but actually just means 'count how many things you have to alter in order to change one pattern into another'. You could, for instance, use this to compare the underlying scripts in Shakespeare with the original stories from which he adapted them, or to compare the scripts for offering hospitality to guests in two different cultures.

As you might suspect, there has been quite a lot of work on using software to model behaviour in this and in other ways. One interesting finding from software modelling is that a lot of apparently complex behaviour can be produced by surprisingly simple underlying causes. Two classic cases are **Simon's ants** (a simple explanation for apparently complex movement by ants) and modelling of **flocking behaviour** in flying birds, schools of fish, etc.

An important concept related to this is **schema theory**. A schema is an underlying template or prototype for something; for instance, the schema for 'sports car' includes the features of being low-slung, and having minimal passenger space. So what? So, this is a bit different from the schema for 'people carrier' which includes the features of being high off the ground, and having lots of passenger space. If you ask someone to tell you the features of a 'good car' then you are likely to hit apparent inconsistencies because 'car' includes the categories of 'sports car' and 'people carrier', each of which has a very different schema from the other. It's a good idea to watch out for issues of this sort when gathering data – you might need to use finer-grained categories (i.e. a more detailed subdivision of categories) than you originally intended.

A closely related concept is **viewpoints**, which in turn are linked to **facet theory**. A respondent might give you completely different responses depending on whether they were answering from their viewpoint as a member of sales staff, or from their other viewpoint as fire officer for the store. Viewpoints are not terribly mathematical, but they do bear a lot of relation to reality. Facet theory is more mathematical, and involves being able to slice things up conceptually in more than one way – for instance, you can categorise animals in terms of what they eat, or in terms of their habitat, or in terms of their Linnaean classification into genus and species. A person may be able to categorise using several facets from within the same viewpoint, so the terms 'viewpoint' and 'facet' aren't synonymous. If you jumble several facets together because of the way you phrase your questions, you can hit problems. For instance, if you ask respondents to say which two animals on a list are 'most similar' without specifying the facet on which you want them to assess similarity, then you'll probably get a mangled pile of miscellaneous grot in response. In the facet of habitat, pine martens live in treetops and sea otters live in the ocean, so they're very dissimilar; in the facet of Linnaean taxonomy, pine martens and sea otters are closely related genetically, so in that sense they're very similar. Facet theory is closely linked to **graph theory**, which we'll cover next.

Graphs and nets

Just as the term 'average' is so useful that it is used with three separate meanings, so the term 'graph' is so useful that it is used with two separate meanings. The most widely known use is 'that thing that you don't confuse with a bar chart'. (Strictly speaking, that is a **line graph**: it's normally abbreviated to 'graph', which is usually fine, but which stores up long-term confusion for anyone who goes on to do more than layperson's stats.) The other use, which is different, is a bit of maths which deals with modelling networks of connections between things. In some fields, such as social geography, networks are well known and widely used. In others, they aren't. Some applications of networks are pretty obvious (for instance, modelling which characters in a Jane Austen novel communicate directly with each other, and which are intermediaries communicating between two otherwise separate groups, such as aristocrats and servants). Others are less obvious. For instance, if you're studying flint artefacts, you can use graph theory to model the network of tools that you need to make the tools to make the tools to make a given artefact (**fabricatory depth**). When I did this for flint axes, one interesting finding (well, interesting to some people) was that the sub-network of tools required to mine high-quality flint for neolithic polished flint axeheads was much bigger than the network of tools required to make the axehead itself from the raw flint. You can do the same thing with **elucidatory depth**, i.e. the layers of explanation required to explain something, as an index of conceptual complexity within a field. In flint artefact classification, for instance, the term 'handaxe' can be explained as 'a bifacially worked tool' and then each term in this explanation can be unpacked in turn; 'bifacially', for instance, means 'on both faces', and 'face' means 'flattish surface'. At this point there's no need to explain the term 'flattish surface', so this branch of the explanation stops after three levels of unpacking. So, what? So this gives you a simple way of measuring complexity in areas where complexity is usually viewed as an intractable can of worms, a topic to which we return soon.

Things to watch out for

There are some apparently innocuous phrases which can leave you wide open to incisive questions from unkind or cynical listeners. This section lists a few of them, in no particular order, to give you the general idea.

'This is very complex.' The surface manifestation may be complex, but that doesn't mean that the underlying cause is complex – **fractals** and **Simon's ants** are fine examples of this principle. There's also an entire branch of mathematics called '**complexity theory**'.

'There are lots of factors involved.' This may provoke a response such as 'Then have you used factor analysis?' There are various areas of statistics and maths, such as **factor analysis** and **principal component analysis**, devoted solely to unpicking the individual factors in multi-factor problems; if you admit that you've never tried using any of these, then it's a bit like saying 'There's lots of things wrong with my car' and admitting that you haven't thought of getting it inspected by a mechanic. There's a chapter on this towards the end of this book.

'A semiotic analysis. . .'. **Semiotics** is an attempt to model meaning in a for-malised, systematic way. Although semiotics looks very impressive at first sight, it is usually based on a highly impoverished form of knowledge representation and measurement theory – typically, binary values such as 'present/absent' or 'raw/cooked'. Also, the categories used in semiotic analyses are usually gener-ated out of the researcher's head, with little or no reference to the categories used by the people being studied. Other approaches have a much richer semantics, and allow you to incorporate the categorisation of the people you're studying. For example, **personal construct theory** is based on finding out how individuals view the world, and on modelling their world-views in a way which is both systematic and as faithful to their idiosyncrasies as possible; it typically uses a rich variety of measurement types and categorisations.

'All explanations are equally valid.' This is the dodgy argument that there's a potentially infinite set of explanations corresponding to a given set of find-ings, therefore all explanations are equally valid. This claim is likely to get short shrift from mathematicians, who know more than most about infinity, and who might point out that there's an infinite number of even numbers, but that this doesn't mean that all numbers are even – there's an equally infinite number of odd numbers, which most definitely aren't even. (There's also an infinite number of prime numbers, for good measure.) This has obvious links with Karl Popper's concept of **falsifiability**. Popper was a philosopher of science who pointed out that what matters is not how much evidence there is in favour of a proposed explanation; what matters is whether or not that proposed explanation is demonstrably wrong. It's like a detective story, where a single piece of evidence can be enough to show that someone definitely didn't commit the crime. As in the Sherlock Holmes story, what you do is to proceed by identifying the key questions which will allow you to eliminate suspects from your enquiries until only the guilty party is left. If it's not possible to answer a particular question, then that question is useless to you, so you choose a question which (a) you can answer and (b) moves you a step nearer to working out who done it. Similarly, if a proposed theory can't be tested and potentially falsified (i.e. shown to be wrong, if it actually is wrong), then it's not much use, and you move on to a different one. For instance, Last Tuesdayism claims that the entire universe was created last Tuesday, complete with memories, records, fossils, etc. It's a fine, rich concept, but impossible to test, and completely useless. The concept of falsifiability fits neatly with stats: statistical tests allow you to test the claim that something is happening other than the random outcomes of chance. I'll resist the temptation to declaim at length about this, and move on.

A parting thought is that you can spare yourself a lot of grief by doing some homework before choosing your research approach. The usual suspects for gathering data from human respondents (i.e. questionnaires and interviews) tend to attract complications like a metal kite in a thunderstorm, and you're often much better off using other techniques, which have the added attraction of earning you a brownie point or two for doing the homework and learning the different tools of your trade. You might, for instance, investigate respondents' categorisation by using **card sorts**, where the respondents categorise things using categories of their own choice, or investigate respondents' use of subjective and idiosyncratic terms by using **laddering**, or investigate gender stereotypes by using **scenarios** in which the gender of the person described is systematically varied. These methods, and more, are well established in various disciplines; at the risk of accusations of nepotism, my book with Marian Petre, *A Gentle Guide to Research Methods*, brings together descriptions of the main methods within one book.

That's a brief skim over the surface of knowledge representation, which might help you avoid comments along the lines of 'I wouldn't have started from here if I were you'. It's a topic well worth investigating, as is the topic of data collection methods, since you can spare yourself a lot of grief by starting from somewhere more amenable. On that encouraging note we'll proceed to a concept deeply embedded in the prototypical schema of every self-respecting statistics book, namely ***probability theory***.

6

The sixfold paths: some observations on probability theory

Randomness • Outcomes • The normal distribution, and its friends and relations • Calculating probabilities: the case of the suspiciously fortunate stranger • Important closing reminder

> *. . . but Jack found that presently he was spreading marmalade upon his turbot and answering somewhat at random.*
>
> (*Master and Commander*, p. 374)

Probability theory sits brooding at the heart of inferential statistics like some Elder God having a bad day. Like Elder Gods having a bad day, probability theory tends to be viewed by students on statistics courses as being enigmatic, inscrutable, and capable of causing them considerable grief, but unlikely to bring much fun to their life. There are various understandable reasons for this. Probability theory involves the concept of randomness, a concept which doesn't feel quite right to most people. It also usually involves decimals, which don't always behave like real proper numbers – for instance, the square root of 4 is a healthy, respectable 2, but the square root of 0.4 is approximately 0.632455 rather than, say, 0.2, which also evokes uneasy feelings in most people. Explanations of probability theory usually involve large numbers of calculations, causing most readers' minds to glaze over. Finally, probability theorists tend to talk about a 'die' where most people would talk about a 'dice', as if to rub in some closing point of pedantic superiority. (Why do they do this? One practical reason is that it reduces the risk of ambiguity when explaining things – there's less risk that the reader will think you mean the dice in the plural, as opposed to one of them in the singular, which is why this book has gone along with this convention.) The consequence of all this is that many people's grasp of probability theory is wobbly at best, and woefully mistaken at worst.

I have no quarrel with the core concepts of probability theory – on the contrary, I think they're a Good Thing. That said, there are a few drawbacks with the usual way of explaining what it's about, so I've used a different way. It ends up in the same place, but involves a slightly different route.

Probability theory is about working out how likely it is that a given thing will happen by chance, such as winning the lottery or having your nuclear power plant explode. The 'by chance' bit is important, and takes us into the concept of randomness, which is where accounts of probability theory traditionally start. It's a sensible tradition, so we'll do the same.

Randomness

The idea of randomness causes existential unease to most people: there's a widespread suspicion that randomness seems to be keeping an unseen eye on the world, making sure that dice in casinos behave themselves and that things form proper statistical distributions just like they ought to. Quite how it can do this is something that most people can't even begin to imagine, so it's scarcely surprising if people also have problems with bits of statistics which include randomness somewhere among their core assumptions.

There is, however, an elegant way of viewing randomness which skirts round these issues. It would be nice to claim that I'd invented it, but it's been floating around for a while, so the credit belongs elsewhere. Anyway, another way to view randomness involves labelling. If you roll a die repeatedly and it shows a 6 most times, then you assume that there's something causing it to do this, and you might do some research to find the cause. If, however, the die tends to show each number equally often, with no bias for or against any number, then it's labelled a fair die, and nobody gives it much more thought. What happens when you roll a fair die? What happens is that a large number of factors affect which way up the die lands. It's usually impossible to measure them because they're so numerous and often tiny. Sometimes there are more leading the die to land on a 6; other times, there are more leading it to land on a 5 or a 1. If there's a systematic tendency for one set of factors to outweigh the others, then we say there's an effect going on. If there isn't a systematic tendency for one set of factors to outweigh the others, then we say that the distribution is random. If you view it this way round, then 'randomness' is just the label we apply to cases where the factors happen to be evenly weighed.

If events are truly random, then this means by definition that it's not possible to predict which particular event out of a set will happen next. That's fairly obvious. However, a less obvious consequence of this is that if you witness a particular event, such as a 6 coming up on a die, then by definition it's not possible to predict which face of the die will come up on the next throw – if you could, it wouldn't be random. So what? So, the outcomes (e.g. a 6 coming up on the die) won't be regularly spaced – you might get two 6s in succession, followed by a long gap with no 6s. In the long run, this will eventually even out: if they didn't even out in the long run, then by definition there would be some sort of systematic bias present, and therefore by the same definition they couldn't be described as 'random'.

In the short run, however, a really random series of events will contain clusters and will also contain gaps, as a necessary consequence of the randomness. Casinos make a lot of money out of having a clear understanding of this; gamblers without a clear understanding of it typically lose a lot of money. What are the implications of randomness? A good question, which leads on to the rest of this section.

Outcomes

The next bit of probability theory involves calculating outcomes from given events, such as rolling a pair of fair dice. It's tempting to assume that all the outcomes are equally likely, but, like many temptations, it's one which ends in tears: the reality is more complex, depending on just what you mean by 'outcome', and this is at the heart of probability theory. The traditional example involves rolling pairs of dice, but that leads to quite a few calculations and to glazed expressions, so I'll illustrate the point instead via the paths to Grandmama's house in the woods.

Figure 6.1 shows paths through the forest. There are six paths, but only three destinations, namely Grandmama's house, the sweet shop and the municipal landfill site; as you might guess, some of the paths converge.

If we now imagine that half a dozen travellers set out, one along each path, how many will reach each destination? It won't be an even distribution, since there are different numbers of paths leading to each destination. Grandmama's house is the destination for three different paths, so she'll get three visitors; the sweet shop is the destination for two different paths, so it will get two potential customers; and the landfill site is reached via one path, so it will get one lucky visitor.

If we now approach the traditional pair of six-sided dice, we can work out the outcomes in the same way as with the routes through the woods, by asking

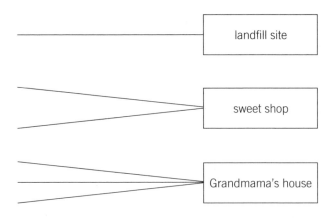

Figure 6.1 Pathways to places

Total score	Ways to get there	No. of routes
2	[1+1]	1
3	[1+2] [2+1]	2
4	[1+3] [3+1] [2+2]	3
5	[1+4] [4+1] [2+3] [3+2]	4
6	[1+5] [5+1] [2+4] [4+2] [3+3]	5
7	[1+6] [6+1] [2+5] [5+2] [3+4] [4+3]	6
8	[2+6] [6+2] [3+5] [5+3] [4+4]	5
9	[3+6] [6+3] [4+5] [5+4]	4
10	[4+6] [6+4] [5+5]	3
11	[5+6] [6+5]	2
12	[6+6]	1

Figure 6.2 Total scores which can be reached with two six-sided dice, and number of ways of reaching each total score

how many destinations there are, and how many ways there are to get to each destination. The destinations are the total scores you get when you add the two dice together.

One thing which sometimes causes problems for people new to statistics is the idea that when you're working out combinations of dice, rolling a 6 plus a 5 is not identical to rolling a 5 plus a 6: although these combinations both give you the same total, they represent two different paths to the same destination. So in order to reduce confusion, we'll assume that one of the dice is red and the other is blue.

The lowest possible score is 2, which you can only reach via the route of getting a 1 on each of the dice. At the other end, the highest possible score is 12, which you can only reach via the route of getting a 6 on each of the dice. Now things start to get more interesting.

The second lowest possible score is 3. You can reach that via two routes. You can either get a 2 on the red die, and a 1 on the blue die, or you can reach it via a 1 on the red die and a 2 on the blue die. When we move on to the next lowest possible score, namely 4, there are even more routes – you can get a 1 on the red die and a 3 on the blue, or a 3 on the red and a 1 on the blue, or a 2 on the red and a 2 on the blue; this means that there are three routes to this score. By the time we get to the total score of 7, there are no less than six possible routes: 1+6, 2+5, 3+4, 4+3, 5+2, 6+1 (see Figure 6.2).

Where does this leave us? If we draw it on a map like the one to Grandmama's house, we start off with a lot of paths, and end up with eleven destinations (the total scores from 2 to 12 inclusive). Some of these destinations can only be reached via one route (i.e. the destination of a total score of 2, and the

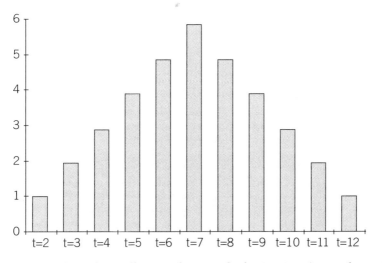

Figure 6.3 Number of travellers reaching each destination (*t* = total number of travellers, assuming two dice)

Total score	Ways to get there	No. of routes
3	[1+1+1]	1
4	[1+1+2] [1+2+1] [2+1+1]	3
5	[1+3+1] [1+1+3] [1+2+2] [2+1+2] [2+2+1] [3+1+1]	6
6	[1+1+4] [1+4+1] [1+2+3] [1+3+2] [2+1+3] [2+3+1] [2+2+2] [3+1+2] [3+2+1] [4+1+1]	10
7	[1+1+5] [1+5+1] [1+2+4] [1+4+2] [1+3+3] [2+1+4] [2+4+1] [2+2+3] [2+3+2] [3+1+3] [3+3+1] [3+2+2] [4+1+2] [4+2+1] [5+1+1]	15
8	[1+1+6] [1+6+1] [1+2+5] [1+5+2] [1+3+4] [1+4+3] [2+1+5] [2+5+1] [2+2+4] [2+4+2] [2+3+3] [3+1+4] [3+4+1] [3+2+3] [3+3+2] [4+1+3] [4+3+1] [4+2+2] [5+1+2] [5+2+1] [6+1+1]	21
9	[1+2+6] [1+6+2] [1+3+5] [1+5+3] [1+4+4] [2+1+6] [2+6+1] [2+2+5] [2+5+2] [2+3+4] [2+4+3] [3+1+5] [3+5+1] [3+2+4] [3+4+2] [3+3+3] [4+1+4] [4+4+1] [4+2+3] [4+3+2] [5+1+3] [5+3+1] [5+2+2] [6+1+2] [6+2+1]	25
10	[1+3+6] [1+6+3] [1+4+5] [1+5+4] [2+2+6] [2+6+2] [2+3+5] [2+5+3] [2+4+4] [3+1+6] [3+6+1] [3+2+5] [3+5+2] [3+3+4] [3+4+3] [4+1+5] [4+5+1] [4+2+4] [4+4+2] [4+3+3] [5+1+4] [5+4+1] [5+2+3] [5+3+2] [6+1+3] [6+3+1] [6+2+2]	27

Figure 6.4 Total scores which can be reached with three six-sided dice, and number of ways of reaching each total score (for scores between 3 and 10)

Total score	Ways to get there	No. of routes
11	[1+6+4] [1+4+6] [1+5+5] [2+3+6] [2+6+3] [2+4+5] [2+5+4] [3+2+6] [3+6+2] [3+3+5] [3+5+3] [3+4+4] [4+1+6] [4+6+1] [4+2+5] [4+5+2] [4+3+4] [4+4+3] [5+1+5] [5+5+1] [5+2+4] [5+4+2] [5+3+3] [6+1+4] [6+4+1] [6+2+3] [6+3+2]	27
12	[1+5+6] [1+6+5] [2+4+6] [2+6+4] [2+5+5] [3+3+6] [3+6+3] [3+4+5] [3+5+4] [4+2+6] [4+6+2] [4+3+5] [4+5+3] [4+4+4] [5+1+6] [5+6+1] [5+2+5] [5+5+2] [5+3+4] [5+4+3] [6+1+5] [6+5+1] [6+2+4] [6+4+2] [6+3+3]	25
13	[1+6+6] [2+5+6] [2+6+5] [3+4+6] [3+6+4] [3+5+5] [4+3+6] [4+6+3] [4+4+5] [4+5+4] [5+2+6] [5+6+2] [5+3+5] [5+5+3] [5+4+4] [6+1+6] [6+6+1] [6+2+5] [6+5+2] [6+3+4] [6+4+3]	21
14	[2+6+6] [3+5+6] [3+6+5] [4+4+6] [4+6+4] [4+5+5] [5+3+6] [5+6+3] [5+4+5] [5+5+4] [6+2+6] [6+6+2] [6+3+5] [6+5+3] [6+4+4]	15
15	[3+6+6] [4+5+6] [4+6+5] [5+4+6] [5+6+4] [5+5+5] [6+3+6] [6+6+3] [6+4+5] [6+5+4]	10
16	[4+6+6] [5+5+6] [5+6+5] [6+4+6] [6+6+4] [6+5+5]	6
17	[5+6+6] [6+5+6] [6+6+5]	3
18	[6+6+6]	1

Figure 6.5 Total scores which can be reached with three six-sided dice, and number of ways of reaching each total score (for scores between 11 and 18)

destination of a total score of 12), while others can be reached by numerous paths (the destination of a total score of 7 can be reached via six different paths). If we now imagine an equal number of travellers setting off along each of these paths, we can draw a histogram of how many reach each destination (see Figure 6.3).

It's apparent from this that some outcomes happen a lot more often than others, because there are more ways of getting to them. You might at this point start wondering what would happen if you added a third die to the calculation. As you might suspect, this leads to more sums, but the outcome is that there's an even wider gap between least frequent destinations and the most frequent. The lowest score becomes 3 (a score of 1 on each of the dice), and it can only be reached via that one route; the number of ways of reaching 7, however, grows considerably more (for instance, you can now reach it via 2+2+3, or via 5+1+1, or via 2+4+1).

For two dice, the number of routes increases or decreases in steps of one route at a time. For three, however, the number of routes now increases or decreases by different amounts each time. Since many people find this hard to imagine, Figures 6.4 and 6.5 show all the possible scores and all the routes to each score, for three six-sided dice.

If you use a histogram to plot the number of routes to each total, you get a curve. Instead of going up one step at a time, as it did for the combinations of two dice, it now goes up unevenly – for instance, there's one way of reaching 3, three ways of reaching 4, and six ways of reaching 5. It starts off slowly, speeds up, then levels off at the top, and then reverses the process on the other side, to form a curve looking a bit like a cross-section of a bell, as shown in Figure 6.6.

As readers who have struggled through other introductions to statistics might suspect, this diagram takes us elegantly into the statistical concept of a *normal distribution*.

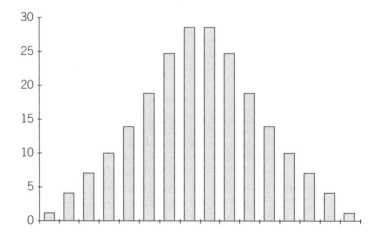

Figure 6.6 Number of routes to each total score for three six-sided dice

The normal distribution, and its friends and relations

Just as numerous different starting points converge to bring you to the same destination in the woods, so numerous different starting points in the world converge to bring you to the same point, in the form of what is often described loosely as a 'normal distribution' (we'll go into a bit more detail later on about what this means). The reason for this convergence is that if you have several different things interacting with each other, each of them contributing variable amounts to some total score, then some of those total scores will be reachable via only one or two routes, whereas others will be reachable in numerous ways. Low scores can only be reached if each of the different things happens to contribute a low score; the converse is true of high scores. Medium-sized total scores, however, can be produced by all sorts of combinations of individual scores. To introduce another simile, it's like collections in the office for a gift when a colleague is leaving. The only way you'll get a miserably ungenerous total in the collection is if everyone gives only a small amount; the only way you'll get an impressively generous collection is if everyone is generous; but in between, you can get a medium-sized collection via numerous permutations of individual generosity, moderation and stinginess. This tendency becomes increasingly pronounced as the number of things increases: the number of routes to the medium scores increases much faster than the number of routes to the low scores or to the high scores. That's probably enough similes for the time being, so we'll now have a look at why statisticians are so immoderately fond of the normal distribution and its kin.

The usual way of showing a normal distribution is as a bell curve, like the one in Figure 6.7. We've used the figures from our histogram for total scores for

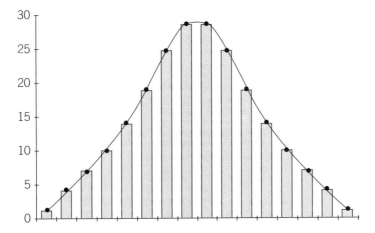

Figure 6.7 Number of routes to each total score for three six-sided dice, with a line graph superimposed, to show the normal distribution emerging

three six-sided dice. The usual convention is to overlay this bell curve with lots of helpful lines, comments and marginalia; the usual reaction from students is the appearance of a glazed expression. Before we go on to a slightly different diagram, a few words of explanation about normal distributions might be helpful.

There are various statistical distributions which are similar in general appearance – a symmetrical bell-shaped curve, but which are not 'normal distributions' in the statistical sense. The details are technical, and life is short, so we won't go into those other distributions; in this book 'normal distribution' is used in the sense defined below.

By definition, a normal distribution has various statistical properties which are very useful. If a distribution turns out not to have those properties, then it isn't a normal distribution, and it's excluded from the statistical equivalent of polite society. One of those useful properties is that the mean, the median and the mode all fall at the same point, right in the middle of the histogram. Another useful property involves the standard deviation, which was discussed long ago in the early part of this book. This property of the normal distribution is that a specified proportion of your sample will fall within one standard deviation of your mean; another specified proportion will fall within two standard deviations, and so on. This can be a bit hard to visualise on a neatly curving line, so it's shown in Figure 6.8 as a blocky histogram instead.

This is what you get if you only use half a dozen histogram bars to show a normal distribution, instead of lots of them. The mean of these scores falls neatly between the two middle bars (together with the median and the mode). The bar to the right of the mean contains the scores up to one standard deviation higher than the mean; the bar to the left of the mean shows the scores up to one standard deviation lower than the mean. Each of these contains

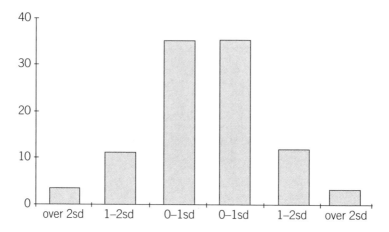

Figure 6.8 A simplified view of a normal distribution (sd = standard deviation)

approximately 34% (rounding off some decimal places) of the cases in your sample (by definition, since if they didn't, it wouldn't be a normal distribution). Combining these together, this means that approximately 68% of your sample will be within one standard deviation of the mean, either above or below it.

The next pair of bars along, the second and fourth, each contain cases which are between one and two standard deviations from your mean. Again, a predictable percentage of your cases will fall into each bar (approximately 13% in each). The last pair of bars, namely the ones at each end, contain cases more than two standard deviations from your mean (about 3%, again with a bit of rounding for simplicity). I haven't shown bars for scores more than three standard deviations from the mean, because there are so few of them (less than 1%).

These insights may leave you less than thrilled, so we'll leave the normal distribution to one side for the time being, and spend some time on the traditional description of calculating dice probabilities. Before we do that, though, we'll pick up some threads from earlier in this section and braid them together. The description of different routes to each destination refers repeatedly to what would happen if the number of travellers along each route were evenly distributed (e.g. one traveller setting out along each route to Grandmama's house in the woods, or one occurrence of each of the possible rolls of the dice). It's important to remember that if you're dealing with random events, such as rolls of unloaded dice, then these will eventually result in even distributions when you have a big enough sample, but they won't usually do this for small samples. For instance, if you roll a pair of dice 36 times, they almost certainly won't happen to turn up each of the 36 possible permutations of the two dice – you'll probably get some permutations turning up two or three times out of the 36, and others not turning up at all. It's an important point, and one which will be laboured at least once more before we move on to some other unfortunate topic. Speaking of which, it's about time for the next section.

Calculating probabilities: the case of the suspiciously fortunate stranger

Observant readers might have noticed that we have made it this far through a chapter on probability theory without doing any arithmetic more complex than adding three 6s together to make 18. Some of these readers might be tempted to start a sweepstake on whether we'll make it to the end of the chapter without doing any multiplication. The answer is that we will indeed be doing some multiplication, since human ingenuity hasn't worked out a way of doing probability theory without some multiplication somewhere.

We'll start by picking up a stray thread from earlier in this chapter, which mentioned somewhat vaguely that there were 'lots of paths' resulting from the combinations of two dice. Just how many? That's where probability theory starts to come in.

If you want to work out the number of combinations that you can get with two different dice, then the procedure is straightforward. Each of the faces on the first die could be combined with each of the faces on the second die. If both have six faces, then each of the six faces on the first die can be combined with each of the six faces on the second die. If you visualise it as six paths starting out from the first die, then each of these paths branches into six further 'second generation' paths, making a total of 36.

It's just a case of multiplying the first number of possibilities by the other number of possibilities. If you want to work out the number of combinations for an eight-sided die and a twelve-sided die, then each of the eight sides on the first die can be combined with each of the twelve sides on the second die; multiplying 8 by 12 gives you 96. What happens if you want to work out the number of possibilities for three dice? It's exactly the same process, except that you're multiplying three numbers together rather than two. So, if you threw a six-sided, an eight-sided and a twelve-sided die at the same time, you would get $6 \times 8 \times 12 = 576$ possibilities.

That basic principle is straightforward, and it allows you to work out things like how many combinations of dice faces you can get. You can use the same principle to calculate the likelihood of a specified set of outcomes on the dice, if you specify accurately enough. So, for instance, if you specify a unique outcome, which can only be reached in one way, then the likelihood of that outcome is one chance out of the total number of possibilities. If you specify, for example, that you want to know the likelihood of getting a 2 on the six-sided die, a 4 on the eight-sided die and a 7 on the twelve-sided die, then there's only one way of getting that, out of 576 possibilities, so the likelihood of that set of scores occcurring is 1/576.

If you want to answer more sophisticated questions, then you need to do some slightly more sophisticated sums. Suppose, for instance, that you've rolled the same three dice, and got a total score of 25; you'd like to know how likely it is that the next person will get an equal or higher score. There's only one way of getting 25 (a 6 plus an 8 plus an 11) out of 576 possible outcomes, and one way of getting the maximum possible score of 26 (a 6 plus an 8 plus a 12) out of 576 possible outcomes. What you do is to add together the likelihood of the first one (the equal score) happening with the likelihood of the second one (the higher score). One chance in 576 plus one chance in 576 gives a total of two chances in 576, i.e. 2/576.

You can do these calculations as decimals, as percentages or as fractions, depending on your preferences. We've used fractions until here because most people find them the easiest method to follow. Around this point, some readers will feel a certain degree of embarrassment, either because they still have some eight-sided dice from their days of role-playing games, or because they thought that adding 1/576 to 1/576 actually gave you 2/1152, so we'll move on to a few improving remarks about base rates and suchlike.

We mentioned the need to specify things carefully, and that's an issue where beginners often encounter bad things. A classic example involves the stranger joining the dice game. There you are, enjoying a sociable game of dice in the bar of the Peyton Farquhar Saloon in Owl Creek, Alabama, when a stranger walks in and asks if he can join the game. You agree, he joins, and he throws a pair of 6s on his first throw. The likelihood of this happening is pretty small – 1/36. However, the likelihood of his throwing any other set of results, such as a 2 on one die and a 4 on the other, is also 1/36. The only reason why anyone pays attention to the pair of 6s is that they have a special significance in the rules, not that they're rarer than any other pair of numbers. (Still on the subject of careful specification, we're talking here about which faces are showing on the dice, not about the total score that those faces add up to.)

Suppose now that the stranger throws again and gets another pair of 6s. The odds against this happening are $1/36 \times 1/36 = 1/1296$. That's a pretty unlikely outcome. However, before anyone gets any ideas about stringing him up from the Owl Creek Bridge, following the deplorable tradition of the region, you might care to reflect that this outcome is again no more unlikely than, say, a 4 plus a 2 on the first roll followed by a 3 and a 1 on the second roll. You might also care to reflect that in the course of a day at the Peyton Farquhar Saloon, the dice are likely to be thrown thousands of times, so you'd expect the occasional one-in-a-thousand outcome to happen anyway: it would be more surprising if you didn't get a one-in-a-thousand outcome at least once per day.

It's advisable to keep this in mind when assessing research findings. If large numbers of researchers do experiments in a given area, then, as a result of sheer chance, at least some of them will find something unlikely. There's a statistical convention that if the likelihood of something happening is less than one in 20, then it's treated as *significant*. What does that mean? It's generally interpreted to mean that there's an initial case for believing that there's a real effect involved, rather than a random fluke. Statisticians in medicine tend to make a distinction between the statistical significance of a result, meaning how likely it is to have occurred by chance alone, and the **clinical significance**, meaning whether it relates to any underlying clinical reality as opposed to random chance. This is a useful distinction, but using the term 'clinical significance' outside the context of medicine can lead to confusion, so I've used 'statistical significance' in a broad sense throughout the book.

The term **null hypothesis** is usually invoked at this point. It's widely used in experimental design, where you start from the null hypothesis that there's actually no difference between two things, such as the success rates of two different teaching methods, and then use statistics to see whether you can disprove the null hypothesis by showing that there actually is a statistically significant difference between them. The trouble is that, for example, if hundreds of True Believers do experiments in the hope that they will prove that Last Tuesdayist medicines cure patients at statistically significant levels, then at least some of them will probably find what appear to be statistically significant results just by chance, regardless of whether the medicines actually work or not, simply because they have run so many experiments. In such cases, as with the dice games in the saloon, you need to look at the wider context to assess what the real likelihood is.

A closing thought involves **confounding factors** and **base rates**. First, confounding factors. The description above deals with working out probabilities if each of the events is unconnected with each of the others – for instance, the two dice aren't joined together in some way. Sometimes things really are unconnected, and you can merrily calculate the likelihood of their co-occurring, with a clear conscience. For instance, whether or not you buy a lottery-winning ticket on a given day is not connected in any obvious way with whether or not you subsequently get struck by a passing meteorite. If you want to calculate the likelihood of being struck by the meteorite on your lucky lottery ticket day, then you simply multiply the likelihood of one by the likelihood of the other.

Other times, though, the two events are connected in some way: sometimes obvious, sometimes less obvious. Suppose, for instance, that you want to calculate the odds of having your alarm clock fail on the same day that you are late for work. It's fairly obvious that having your alarm clock fail would be pretty directly connected to whether or not you were late for work, and would increase the likelihood of being late. How much would it increase it? That's a more complicated question, and questions of this sort are often difficult to answer, which is why astute researchers are careful to ask clean questions if they can, where 'clean' means 'capable of being answered fairly unequivocally'.

In the world, a lot of things are interconnected, often in ways which look unlikely at first sight, so some outcomes will tend to happen a lot more often than would be expected from a naïve calculation of probabilities. When two or more things are intertwined with each other in this way, they're often referred to as *confounding factors*, not to mention various other and less respectable names; much of experimental design exists with the sole purpose of unconfounding them. It's not always easy, but it can usually be done with a certain amount of ingenuity; that, however, is another issue, which we'll leave to one side for the time being.

A closely related issue involves what are known as **base rates** in some disciplines, and **prevalence** in others (including statistics – I've used 'base rates' because it's one that readers of this book are more likely to have met in their pre-statistical days). A base rate is a description of how widespread something is: for instance, the base rate of left-handedness in the British adult population is about 10%. The base rate can often be modified by some factor; in the case of left-handedness, the incidence of practising left-handedness is higher among younger people, since it's not discouraged as much nowadays as was the case in previous years. As you might imagine, base rates are very useful things to know if you're dealing with applications of statistics in real life, such as working out the incidence of various types of road accident.

So, for instance, you might find that large numbers of accidents occur while the driver is using a mobile phone. It's plausible that using a mobile phone might distract the user's attention and cause an accident, but unless you know the base rate of mobile phone use among drivers, you can't draw many conclusions. If almost everyone used mobile phones almost continuously while driving, then it would scarcely be surprising if a lot of accidents occurred while the driver was on the phone. If, on the other hand, the base rate was much lower – a few per cent of drivers using phones, and then only for a few minutes on each journey – then a high association between mobile phone use and accident rates would be much more interesting. All well and good, but in reality it is often difficult to obtain accurate data for base rates, which means that human beings and statisticians often have to do the best they can with imperfect and incomplete data. As with confounding variables, there are ways of working round this, but that's another story, and again involves research methods rather than statistics in the strict sense. We'll return to this in the closing chapter.

Important closing reminder

Randomness is a key concept in statistics. It also has some sneaky, counter-intuitive habits. One thing which is particularly sneaky is that *random distributions* are not the same as *even distributions* – in fact, if you're dealing with smallish samples, then random distributions will almost certainly be uneven. What does this mean? It means that if, for instance, you're plotting a map of where rare and essentially random events happen, such as gas explosions in inner London or people being killed by falling trees in a rural part of the country, then the map will almost certainly show clusters, purely as a result of randomness. It's extremely unlikely that rare events will form an even distribution (e.g. one per square on your map); what you'd expect instead is some squares which are empty, some which have one or two entries, and a few squares with several entries. That's why arrivals of buses and other rare events seem to happen in clusters – if they're random, then they really will quite often happen in clusters. As your sample size increases, so the data will tend to even out, but for small samples, you'll probably get at least some random clumping. How do you tell the difference between a cluster due to randomness and a cluster due to an effect? That's a good question, and, as you might suspect, it leads on to the rest of this book.

It's now time to turn to the next topic, namely inferential statistics.

7

Inferential statistics: some introductory thoughts

Phrasing your research question correctly – a very important bit • Varieties of inferential statistics • Choosing statistical tests: a first encounter • Using statistical tests: some points about the following chapters

> *. . . he began to read into the odd angles a mathematical significance which seemed to offer vague clues regarding their purpose.*
>
> (*The Dreams in the Witch-House*, p. 308)

Classic story plots have a long history, of variable degrees of honour. Some plots, such as arrogance followed by downfall, are at the heart of some of the greatest tragedy ever written. Others, such as the albino minstrel who turns out to be the werewolf, are less widely used. One recurrent theme in the darker areas of invention is the Faustian pact, where the protagonist is offered a set of wishes which lead ultimately to destruction. If you're in the middle of your final-year project, trying to get your data to make sense, then you might well understand that temptation all too clearly: if someone offered you an instant answer, you'd be strongly tempted to sign on the dotted line and ignore the fine print plus the smell of sulphur.

Few characters in such stories stop to think about the nature of the answer that they're looking for. This might be because they're that sort of person; it might be that the story wouldn't last very long if they did. Setting aside the literary implications for the moment, this strategy can be helpful with a common problem facing researchers new to statistics, namely how to use inferential statistics. If you look a couple of jumps ahead, and imagine that you've finally obtained the answer that you've been struggling towards, then you can ask yourself whether that answer will give you what you were looking for in the first place, or whether it will give you something different.

Imagine, as a hypothetical instance, that you've noticed an apparent correlation between two factors, such as amount of halibut eaten and happiness. You make this the topic of your final-year project. You gather large quantities of data and analyse it. What would you expect the answer to look like? What it will actually look like is a number from the stats test, telling you how strong the correlation is on a scale from −1 to +1. Suppose it tells you that there's a correlation of 0.74 – quite a strong positive correlation. So what? What are you going to do with that information? It's pretty limited in its implications, and you can't even be sure of the direction of causality: it might be that eating halibut makes people happier, but (as anyone who has eaten much halibut will probably agree) this isn't a terribly plausible hypothesis. It might be that happy people are more likely to eat halibut, perhaps because the body's homeostatic systems have kicked in to prevent an overload of joy; it might also be that the halibut and the happiness are both consequences of the same underlying cause, such as being a client of the cheerful fishmonger on Innsmouth Street. Correlations won't tell you which is the case; to investigate these possibilities, you'd need to do a different type of study, such as a formal experiment where you feed people halibut, assuming that you could get it past the ethics committee.

So, what are the answers that inferential statistics might give you, what questions do they answer, and what can you do with them? For that matter, you might be trying to remember what inferential statistics are anyway. A brief reminder: descriptive statistics are for describing your findings; inferential statistics are for making inferences about your findings.

With correlations, the answer was: 'here is the amount of correlation between the things you asked about'. If you want to find out whether two or more variables co-vary with each other, either positively or negatively, then correlations can give you an answer. What can you do with it? Usually, you can use it to establish an initial case for a further bit of study.

One answer that inferential statistics can give you is similar to the one about correlations: 'here's the strength of association between these two things'. Another, usually more useful one, is: 'here's the likelihood that your results are the product of random chance'. You might, for instance, find that your high-halibut respondents are all much more cheerful than the no-halibut ones; inferential statistics might then tell you that there's only one chance in a thousand that this is a result of coincidence (e.g. the chance that all of the halibut people happened to have a good day simultaneously because of numerous separate things utterly unrelated to the diet).

Neither of these answers says anything about proving that one thing causes another. In the golden age of science fiction, eminent professors would Prove Things through Science (and a very useful plot device it was too, allowing the story to get on to the special effects more quickly), but that's not how contemporary research works. Over the last fifty years or so, there's been a growing acceptance that empirical, evidence-based research can only be a series of best approximations, reached by eliminating the impossible and then choosing whichever of the remaining possible explanations corresponds most closely to what we can observe. Some of these approximations are extremely good approximations – at an everyday level, gravity behaves very much as predicted by the current best explanation. Others are a bit more wobbly: for instance, our best approximations about how gravity behaves at extremely short or long distances could do with some improvement.

Put another way, in the Past a lot of people tried to use research methods to prove things; now, people use research methods to eliminate some of the possible explanations, and then see what's left. If you've done your homework properly, and chosen your topic carefully, then there might only be two or three possible explanations that anyone considers to be serious contenders – this is where reading the right literature, such as recent journal articles on the topic, can make your life much happier. If you phrase your research question correctly, then you might well be able to eliminate all but one of these possible explanations, leaving the remaining one as the only plausible explanation for the phenomenon in question. How do you eliminate a possible explanation? Usually you can't absolutely eliminate it, but what you can do with inferential statistics is to assess how unlikely it is. If there's only a one in a million chance that one explanation matches the facts, and there's a one in two chance that an alternative explanation matches the facts, then it's pretty clear which is the more plausible explanation.

Phrasing your research question correctly – a very important bit

In an ideal world, you'd be able to find a direct answer to every question you wanted to ask; this, however, is not an ideal world. More usually, you have to ask a series of questions, with each of these giving you another piece of the puzzle, until you finally have all the pieces you need. It's much like a classic whodunnit detective story, where the detective wants to know who killed Colonel Mustard in the dining room with the candlestick. It's not terribly likely that the murderer will immediately volunteer the information that they done it. What the detective has to do instead is to work out a successive set of questions and answers, each moving a step closer to the final piece of the puzzle. The footprints on top of the bookcase show that the murderer was of no more than average height; the hair in the stuffed heron's beak shows that the murderer had dyed black hair; the only person in the rectory matching that description was the butler, therefore the detective can conclude that the butler done it.

It's similar with inferential statistics. You might not be immediately able to answer the question that you'd really like to answer, but you can use inferential statistics to help you find an answer that gets you most of the way towards the answer that you really want. To make best use of inferential stats, it's useful to know what types of question you can answer with them.

Most of these questions are variants on a theme. That theme is: 'How likely is it that these results are due to nothing more than the ordinary variation that you'd get by random chance if there was no systematic effect present?' That's where research design comes in: if you design your research correctly, then it helps you to eliminate the overwhelming majority of possible explanations, and to put some solid numbers on the ones that remain.

Varieties of inferential statistics

So, back to the main theme of this chapter. Descriptive statistics allow you to describe your data, but don't allow you to answer the 'so what?' question (i.e. 'You have this finding – so what?'). Inferential statistics allow you to answer the 'so what?' question by saying what the likelihood is of your findings being the result of random chance. That may not bring as much satisfaction as hurling the villain from the highest parapet at the end of the duel scene, but in research terms it's a lot better than nothing. As with most Good Things, inferential statistics come in several main varieties and numerous sub-varieties; the following chapters describe the main varieties and, as an added bonus, also describe ways of measuring correlation.

Inferential statistics fall into one or other of two categories, with a commendable absence of fuzziness. Which branch of the statistical path do you follow for your data? That depends on the sort of data that you have. If your data form a normal distribution, then you use what are called *parametric statistics*; if not, you use *non-parametric* statistics.

Some classic uses of inferential statistics include the following. You might be testing whether the group that you're studying (limpets in the rock pool, for instance) are larger on average than you'd expect within the bounds of random variation within the limpet population, and might therefore be a new species. You might be testing whether the new method that West and Walsh have developed for reintegrating offenders into the community produces any better results than the traditional methods. You might be testing whether a particular subset of the population are disproportionately likely to be unemployed, or to be dentists.

Some of these things involve comparing two or more groups against each other (for instance, your subset of the population and the population at large). Some involve assessing the effects of an intervention, such as using the West and Walsh rehabilitation method and seeing what happens. This technique of altering one thing and seeing what effect that has on another thing is technically known as **manipulating the independent variable** and observing its effect on the **dependent variable**. There are also questions such as how you tell whether or not your sample forms a normal distribution in the first place, which you can also test using inferential statistics. It's a fine, rich world to explore, though there's a strong argument for exploring it a bit at a time, rather than trying to rush through all of it in one go.

What you'll end up with after using inferential statistics is a probability estimate. If you phrase your research question carefully, then this gives you two possible outcomes, as follows (though you should be aware that using the phrasings below for your write-up would be a rather bad idea).

1 'Wow, this is statistically significant!'
2 'Wow, this isn't statistically significant!'

What does this mean? The 'statistically significant' bit means 'the likelihood of this having happened just through random chance is less than one in 20'. That level of chance is the one conventionally agreed to be the boundary between chance on the one hand, and an initial case for there being something non-random occurring, on the other hand. (Important bit of clarification: statistical significance at the 0.05 level doesn't prove that there's a real effect; it just shows that there's a strong enough case for you to be justified in thinking that there might be a real effect.) The 'Wow!' bit is also important. If you're doing research, rather than just looking for evidence which agrees with your prejudices or your hunches, then the smart thing to do is to ask a question where all the possible answers are interesting for some reason. If you do that, then every piece of research you do should produce an interesting outcome, and help you towards fortune, glory, or whichever other goals are important to you. If you don't do that, then sooner or later you're going to find a boring answer, and everyone including yourself will wonder why you bothered wasting time on that bit of research. Asking the right research question is a learned skill, and a key skill if you want to be a good researcher; the details are outside the scope of this book, but you can find more about this in most good books on research methods.

At first sight, finding that something isn't statistically significant might appear to be something of a non-result. Not so. If you ask the right research question, then a result which finds no statistical significance can be very useful. In an early chapter, we used the hypothetical case of the medieval doctor treating your smallpox by draping the room in red cloth. This is an example where the 'no statistical significance' finding could be very useful: if you could show that there was no statistically significant difference between the recovery rates of patients in rooms draped with red cloth, and patients in rooms not draped with red cloth, then that would strongly suggest that the red cloth wasn't helping patients recover, and could probably be consigned to the rubbish bin of medical history.

Choosing statistical tests: a first encounter

Statistical tests are very useful tools, but, like physical tools such as spanners and pliers, there's an apparently bewildering variety of them, and choosing the appropriate variety is important. If you try to undo a metric nut with an imperial spanner, or to cut a mortise hole with a gouge, then it will end in tears. The same goes for choice of statistical test. At best, using the wrong test will involve you in a lot of wasted effort; at worst, it could give misleading results, and lead to your being mocked in print by more knowledgeable people. In some extreme cases, misunderstanding results has led to tragedy – the wrong person convicted of a crime, because forensic evidence involving probability was misunderstood, or patients being operated on unnecessarily by surgeons who didn't understand the probability of the patient having cancer versus the probability of the diagnostic test giving a wrong result, or patients dying because the supposed treatment was actually more likely to make them worse than to help them recover. It's therefore a wise idea to take statistical advice before firming up your research design, so you can be sure that you're planning to use the right approach. It will also usually allow you to work more efficiently, and to get more out of the same amount of effort.

On that stirring note, what are the issues involved in choosing a statistical test? There are several. In no particular order, they include the following. We'll return to each of them in more detail when discussing the various families of tests.

What measurement type is involved? The choice of test is strongly affected by whether your data are nominal, ordinal, interval, or ratio measurements. Usually the nearer you are to having ratio measurements, the more powerful the tests you can use (and therefore the less data you need to scrape through your project if you're of an indolent disposition, or the more you can do with a given quantity of data if you're keen on asking big questions).

Normally distributed or not? If you're dealing with data which are, or which should be, normally distributed, then you can use one family of tests, known as parametric statistics. How can you tell if your data *are* normally distributed? There are statistical tests which allow you to answer this question. How can you tell if your data *should be* normally distributed? That's something that you can extract from the literature. For instance, the literature might make it pretty obvious that a particular characteristic is normally distributed throughout the relevant population – for example, shoe sizes or potato weights.

Same sample sizes or not? In some cases, your research involves two or more groups which you are comparing. As you might suspect, you can use more powerful statistical tests if the groups are the same size as each other. You can still do some statistical tests even if the groups are different sizes, which is often the case for reasons outside your control, but if you have any choice, then going for same-sized groups is usually a good idea.

There are also some questions which apply specifically to statistics used in conjunction with a formal experimental design, where you're assigning subjects to groups, manipulating variables, and so forth.

Within-subject or between-subjects design? In some research, you reuse the same subjects – for instance, asking each respondent to listen to two different pieces of music. This is known as a **within-subject design**. In other cases, you don't, and you use different subjects for the different tasks – for instance, asking each respondent in group A to listen to one piece of music, and asking each respondent in group B to listen to a different piece of music. This is known as a **between-subjects design**. Within-subject designs have the great advantage that reusing the same person means that there shouldn't be much variation between that person when listening to their first bit of music, and that same person when listening to the other bit of music. You don't need to worry about whether you just happen to have got a bunch of tone-deaf philistines in group A, and a bunch of decadent aesthetes in group B, which might arguably have some effect on their subjective ratings of the music: this sort of worry is a perennial hassle in between-groups designs. In within-subject designs, each respondent judges both bits of music, so there aren't any between-groups differences to allow for.

Why would anyone in their senses use a between-groups design, in light of this? Sometimes you don't have any choice because of the nature of the question. Suppose, for instance, that you want to compare how well children learn to read using either of two different methods. If you try to teach a child using each method in sequence, the unfortunate infant will probably become mightily confused because the two methods clash with each other, and will perform worse with the second method you use, whichever it is. For research questions of this sort, where what you did to the subjects before will affect how they perform this time, you'll usually have to use a between-subjects design. If you have any choice, then a within-subject design is usually more advisable, but you'll need to remember things like counterbalancing the order of presentation (e.g. having half the respondents listen to the Abba music clip first and the New Order clip second, and having the other half listen to New Order before Abba, in case there's a systematic tendency for respondents to behave differently as time goes by, because of factors such as boredom).

One variable or more? Sometimes you're manipulating one *independent variable* at a time in an experiment: for instance, you vary the tempo of the background music while respondents are doing a task, and see whether the tempo affects the speed with which the respondents perform the task. Sometimes you try to answer several questions at once, for instance by varying both the room temperature and the tempo of the background music, to see how much effect each has on the dependent variable, and how much they interact with each other – for instance, do subjects perform much worse with high temperature and fast tempo than in any other combination of conditions? Your choice of test will be affected by the number of things that you're varying.

One condition or more? If you're manipulating variables, sometimes you can manipulate them on a continuous scale, as with tempo and temperature above. Other times, this isn't possible. For instance, you might be manipulating the variable of 'indoors or outdoors setting', in which case there's a pretty limited number of options. Another frequently used approach is to use just two or three settings of a continuous variable, such as temperature – for instance, a high temperature, a medium temperature and a low temperature. This often makes the experimental design simpler than having lots of different temperatures, and also often allows you to use fewer subjects. If there are no differences in results from the three settings of high, medium and low, then there's not much point in looking into temperature in more detail; if there are differences, then the three settings might well tell you everything that you need to know.

Using statistical tests: some points about the following chapters

Many students view manuals of statistical tests as being very similar to grimoires of unhallowed knowledge or folk dancing, involving inscrutable rituals that have to be followed regardless of whether the words make any sense, and usually involving slaughtering a chicken or pulling your partner's moustache somewhere in the proceedings. The following chapters explain the underlying principles of each family of statistical test, and give a worked example of a test from each family, to demonstrate just what the test does. They also include a couple of sections showing how you could do a specified test by hand, if you felt so inclined – you don't have to read these, but it would be good for you to give it a try. I have included these sections because (a) some readers might like to know the underlying technicalia and (b) because technical bits are part of the schema for any self-respecting stats book, and I'd never hear the last of it from reviewers if I didn't include them. Where the technical explanations underpinning the calculations are too complex to be easily explained in the space available, I have given a brief, simple explanation which contains a reasonable amount of truth.

On a similar principle, I haven't described all the tests within a particular family; I've usually described one test, as a demonstration of the key features which are particular to that family.

A minor point of phrasing: I've avoided using the word 'subject' where possible, for the simple reason that it's ambiguous – it may be used to mean 'topic' or to mean 'respondent', both of which are mentioned frequently. The current convention in social sciences is to call respondents 'participants' rather than 'subjects'; in case that wasn't confusing enough, most stats books and packages, and some other disciplines, will use the word 'subjects'. When referring to a consenting human who is giving you information, I've used 'respondent', and for other purposes, I've used 'subject'.

Our closing thought is that when using statistics, it's highly advisable to work backwards from where you want to end up. Imagine you've got your answer, and imagine how you would use it; then find out what sort of statistical test would give you that type of answer, and from that work out what sort of research design would allow you to use that sort of statistical test. One point relating to this is that, for the examples which follow, we'll assume for simplicity that you're performing what is known as a one-tailed test, i.e. testing whether your variables differ in a particular direction which you've specified in advance, rather than a two-tailed test, where you hedge your bets by simply testing whether they're different in any direction. (This will all make more sense later – it's mentioned here primarily as a reassurance to readers who have already learned some stats elsewhere, and who might otherwise be wondering whether I'd forgotten to include this topic, or whether they'd imagined it.)

On that note, we will end this chapter, and proceed to the next. The next chapter is about non-parametric statistics. It's usually possible to do these quite easily with pen, paper and pocket calculator, though you can use a stats package if you prefer. I've shown the calculations involved, to explain the underlying principles. It's worth bearing in mind that different calculators and different stats packages may give slightly different values after the first few decimal points, because of issues such as how they handle rounding, so if you try working through the examples yourself, you might get subtly different results. So it goes.

8

Non-parametric statistics

The case of the unequal tiddlywinks set • Some closing thoughts • Meeting the family

> *... his deep, hollow voice ... bellowed out the opening words of a terrible formula.*
>
> (*The Case of Charles Dexter Ward*, p. 300)

Sometimes in life you don't have a lot of options available. After Napoleon's army had won the battle of Marengo, his cook was, according to legend, faced with the challenge of preparing a meal worthy of the First Consul out of an improbable selection of ingredients which were all that he had been able to scrounge, and succeeded magnificently by inventing chicken Marengo. He'd almost certainly have been a lot happier, though, if he'd had a more orthodox set of ingredients available.

It's similar with statistics. You do what you can to get as near as possible to ratio or at least interval measurements, but sometimes the need for validity or the nature of the problem leaves you with no option but to use nominal categories. For instance, if you're surveying the types of arthropod in your square metre of forest on a field trip, then each type of arthropod is a separate nominal category, and that's the way things are. All, however, is not lost; as with the chicken Marengo, you can still do useful things with such data. That's where non-parametric statistics come to the rescue, like the 'unorthodox chicken recipes' pages in your metaphorical cookbook.

Non-parametric statistics are a tolerant set of statistical tests, which don't

expect your data to be anything fancy, and which can handle nominal categories: a bit like an easy-going uncle who will accept that you are human and
imperfect. Also like a typical easy-going uncle, they're not high-powered, and
they don't promise more than they can deliver.

As with all types of statistical test, the best way to view them is as a way of
finding out how likely it is that your findings can be accounted for by nothing
more than simple random chance. What the tests do is to work out how often
random chance would produce results matching those in your data. How, you
might wonder rhetorically, do they do that? The traditional metaphor at this
point involves flipping coins, but that metaphor has earned a brief rest, so
we'll look instead at tiddlywinks.

Tiddlywinks, for those who have led a sheltered life, is a sport which
involves a moderate number of counters, usually made of plastic, about the
size of small coins. You press the edge of one counter hard against the edge of
another, which makes the second counter skip through the air. The general
objective is to flip all of your counters into a small pot, used as a target, before
your opponent; there are numerous variants on the game.

If we imagine that you are a complete beginner at tiddlywinks, your aim
might initially be no better than random chance. In this case, if you had two
equal-sized pots next to each other, each counter that you flipped would be
equally likely to land in either pot. If you flipped two hundred counters, you'd
expect about a hundred to land in each pot. About, but not exactly . . . We'll
start with your first counter. There's one chance in two that it will land in
the left-hand pot (we'll assume from now on that any counters which miss the
pots are flipped again until they do go in, otherwise this chapter would be
twice its present length). What about the second counter? There's also one
chance in two that it will land in the left-hand pot; the same goes for the third
counter, and the fourth, and all the others.

If we do some brief calculations, the likelihood of two consecutive counters
both going into the left-hand pot is one in two multiplied by one in two,
namely one in four. Another way of viewing it is to list all the pathways,
thus:

- first counter in left pot, second counter in left pot;
- first counter in left pot, second counter in right pot;
- first counter in right pot, second counter in left pot;
- first counter in right pot, second counter in right pot.

If we add in the pathways for a third counter, then we get Figure 8.1, showing the pathways and the number of counters which end up in each pot. I've
given an arbitrary name to each route, to make things easier in the following
description.

So, if we flip three counters, it's possible that all three will go into the
same pot, but it's not very likely – there's one chance in eight that they'll all go
into the left pot (route A), and one chance in eight that they'll all go into the

Distribution	No. in left pot	No. in right pot	Route name
first in left pot, second in left pot, third in left pot	3	0	A
first in left pot, second in left pot, third in right pot	2	1	B
first in left pot, second in right pot, third in left pot	2	1	C
first in right pot, second in left pot, third in left pot	2	1	D
first in right pot, second in left pot, third in right pot	1	2	E
first in right pot, second in right pot, third in left pot	1	2	F
first in left pot, second in right pot, third in right pot	1	2	G
first in right pot, second in right pot, third in right pot	0	3	H

Figure 8.1 Tiddlywinks outcomes

right pot (route H), but there's six chances out of eight that they won't all go into the same pot. As you might suspect, the more counters you flip, the lower the relative likelihood that all the counters will go into one pot. With three counters, there's only one chance in eight that all the counters will go into the left pot, for instance; with four counters, there's only one chance in 16 that all of them will go into the left pot, and by the time you're dealing with seven counters, there's only one chance in 128 that they'll all go into the left pot.

So far, that's basic probability theory, which is by no means to be sniffed at; you can do a lot of interesting and useful things with what we've done so far in this chapter. Suppose, for instance, that you are studying a sports club consisting of seven extreme sports enthusiasts, and you notice that all seven are male. If we assume that the proportion of males to females in the general population is even (to make the maths a bit gentler on readers) then we can ask what the odds are against all seven people in the club happening to be male. The two categories of 'males in the general population' and 'females in the general population' are the same size as each other, just as our two tiddlywinks pots are the same size as each other, and we can calculate the pathways in just the same way. For a two-member club, for instance, the pathways are shown in Figure 8.2.

That's a one in four chance of both members in the two-member club being male, just as there's a one in four chance of both counters in a two-tiddlywink game being in the left pot. Also as in the tiddlywink example, the likelihoood of all seven being in the same category, namely male, is one in 128.

What happens if you have more than two categories? It's exactly the same principle, except that the number of pathways gets a lot bigger. If you have three pots, for instance, there's a one in three chance that your first counter

| first member male, second member male |
| first member male, second member female |
| first member female, second member male |
| first member female, second member female |

Figure 8.2 Two-member club pathways

will go in the middle pot, and the likelihood of both the first counter and also the second counter going into the middle pot is one in three multiplied by one in three, i.e. one in nine.

You could, if you felt so inclined, work out all the pathways that fitted your particular case, but most people prefer to use software and/or tables which have already worked out the pathways for you. This is particularly handy if you're not looking at a simple case. For some cases, such as the likelihood of the first four counters all ending up in the middle one of the three pots (or all eight members of the group you're studying happening to be from the same school out of the three schools in the town), calculating the likelihood is straightforward. For more realistic cases, such as the likelihood of six out of the eight members of the group happening to be from the same school out of three in the town, the calculation gets a bit tedious if you do it by hand.

The case of the unequal tiddlywinks set

So far, we've been looking at a simplified version of reality. In the real world, tiddlywinks sets usually have some counters missing, and you're unlikely to find two identical-sized tiddlywinks pots when the urge to play strikes you at midnight after a litre of wine in the local bodega – more likely you'll find the set contains 12 red counters and 18 green ones, and that the nearest approximation to a second pot you can find is a plastic container on the washing-up rack that's twice the size of the official tiddlywinks pot. In your research, the equivalent might be that you're looking at the distribution of different animal bones between different sized pits on an archaeological site, or you're comparing pay rates among graduates from six different schools in two different counties, with different numbers of graduates emerging from each school. As before, statistics can come to the rescue, via some slightly more fiddly calculations.

Unequal-sized pots

We'll start with the simple case of two unequal-sized pots, and then progress to the case of two unequal-sized pots combined with different numbers of red and green counters. After that, we'll reflect on how this corresponds to non-parametric statistical tests.

Following a long and honourable tradition, we'll make an initial assumption which will keep the calculations within decent bounds: we'll assume that the improvised pot has a mouth with exactly twice the surface area of the proper pot. This means that if we flip counters randomly at the two pots, then for every counter that goes into the smaller, proper pot, about two counters should go into the bigger, improvised pot. Scaling up the numbers a bit, if 10 counters went into the smaller pot, then about 20 counters should go into the other pot, with twice as big a mouth. But what does 'about 20' mean if you translate it into actual numbers? Again, we can calculate this via the possible paths, though we need some way of allowing for the fact that one pot is twice as big as the other.

There are various ways of representing the different sizes of the pots. Probably the simplest is to think of the bigger pot as consisting of two halves called A and B, and then treat each of these as if it was a pot. That turns this into the same situation as we encountered when dealing with the pathways for three pots, except that we need to remember to add together the results for the two halves of the bigger pot. The individual bits of the calculation are pretty straightforward, but there are quite a lot of individual bits, and the novelty of working out the combinations soon wears thin. Figure 8.3 shows the pathways for a couple of counters flipped at the proper pot and the big pot. It uses the sigma symbol (Σ) to show the totals, as is usual in statistics.

Of these nine pathways, only one involves both counters ending up in the small pot; two pathways involve both counters ending up in the big pot, and the six remaining pathways involve one counter ending up in each pot. There are six paths which lead into the smaller pot, and 12 (i.e. twice as many) leading into the bigger pot, as we'd expect. You can work out the pathways for other combinations of pot sizes (e.g. one pot which has four times the surface area of the other) in just the same way, and mightily tedious it is too; the principle, however, is quite straightforward. So, for instance, if one school in the town has twice as many pupils as the other, but the two pupils with the highest exam scores both come from the smaller school, this is exactly the same underlying situation as two counters both landing in the smaller of our two pots, and the likelihood of its being due to chance is one in nine.

Different numbers of counters

The previous subsection described how to calculate the likelihood of counters going into different-sized pots. What happens if you're using one pot, but you're using two lots of counters, and there's twice as many of one colour as of

First counter	Second counter	Total in small pot	Total in big pot
small pot	small pot	2	0
small pot	big pot (A)	1	1
small pot	big pot (B)	1	1
big pot (A)	small pot	1	1
big pot (A)	big pot (A)	0	2
big pot (A)	big pot (B)	0	2
big pot (B)	small pot	1	1
big pot (B)	big pot (A)	0	2
big pot (B)	big pot (B)	0	2
		$\Sigma = 6$	$\Sigma = 12$

Figure 8.3 Paths for two counters going into two different-sized pots

the other? You might be gratified to hear that it's exactly the same underlying problem as the two different-sized pots, and you solve it in just the same way, with 'colour' replacing 'size' in the assorted tables and suchlike. You might be even more gratified to hear that we won't repeat the assorted tables; if you're not quite sure how to work out the likelihoods for different coloured counters, and you're feeling conscientious, then you can draw up your own table and work out the combinations. If you have twice as many green counters as red ones, then you might find it useful to work with one red counter, and two green counters labelled green (A) and green (B) so you can tell them apart.

Different-sized pots and different numbers of counters

The most complicated case is when you're dealing both with different-sized pots and with different numbers of colours simultaneously. You might, for instance, be an archaeologist trying to compare the relative proportions of different types of pottery fragments in two pits of different sizes; you might be a sociologist trying to compare the relative proportions of people from different ethnic backgrounds who went to each of several different public schools; you might be a biologist looking at the population sizes of each of several species of arthropod in several different-sized ponds. It's even more interesting when you don't know exactly how big the pots are. How do you set about calculating whether one group is disproportionately rare, or whether another group is disproportionately common? It's the same underlying problem as calculating likely outcomes from different-sized pots and different colours of counters.

It is possible to represent the outcomes as a set of pathways, but the resulting table would be hideously big, and would probably include an origami exercise where you folded the table into six-dimensional space. The underlying concepts are very simple, but the number of steps and calculations involved can be a bit much. It's an example of the snowflake principle: each individual snowflake is tiny and easy to deal with, but when you encounter several million of them simultaneously in an avalanche, it's a bit overwhelming.

You might, therefore, be relieved to know that there are shorter ways of handling the problem, in the form of assorted non-parametric statistical tests. These typically involve a limited amount of division and subtraction, plus reference to a table which someone else has already worked out. We'll go through how one of these tests works, to illustrate the general idea.

A worked example: the case of the incognito tiddlywinker

You might by this stage be wondering why anyone should be using more than one tiddlywinks pot. It's a fair question. To add some gritty realism, we'll imagine that you're having a game of competitive tiddlywinks against someone that you met on your evening out, with one of the pots being the real target, and the other pots next to it being the equivalent of ponds on a golf course – any counters that go into them have to stay in them, and don't count as a score. The stranger has the red counters, and you have the green counters. The underlying principle for the statistics is gentle and straightforward.

- You allow for one pot containing more counters than the other.
- You also allow for one colour of counter being more common than the other.
- You work out how many of each colour you would expect to find in each pot if the counters were shared out evenly in light of those allowances.
- You work out the difference between these expected numbers and the numbers that you've actually got.
- Finally, you look up that difference in a table, which tells you how likely it is that a difference of that size is due to nothing more than chance.

For clarity and simplicity, we've used the example of three pots and only two colours. One pot is square, one is oval and one is round; there are 60 red counters and 104 green counters. At the end of the tiddlywinks game, there are 16 red counters and 80 green counters in the square pot, 8 red and 4 green in the oval pot, and 36 red and 20 green in the round pot. How likely is it that these results are the result of random chance?

Having by now become inured to drawing tables, we'll start by drawing one to show the distributions of counters at the end of the game (Figure 8.4).

The next step is to work out how many counters of each colour you would

	Square pot	Oval pot	Round pot	Σ
Red counters	16	8	36	60
Green counters	80	4	20	104
Σ	96	12	56	164

Figure 8.4 Observed frequencies of counter distributions

expect to see in each pot if they were evenly distributed. If you start with the red counters in the square pot, then you need to allow for the number of red counters as a proportion of the total number of counters, and you also need to allow for the number of counters of either colour in the square pot, which contains more counters than the other two pots put together. The short way to do this is to multiply the total number of red counters (60) by the total number of counters in the square pot (96), and then divide the resulting number (5760) by the total number of counters (164). The result is 35.12. This means that we would expect to see 35.12 red counters in the square pot if they were proportionately distributed. We can repeat the process for the other five combinations of counter colour and pot shape, multiplying the total number of relevant-coloured counters by the total number of counters in the relevant pot shape, and dividing the result by the total number of counters of both colours. This gives us Figure 8.5, which shows the expected values if you and your opponent were scoring at the level of random chance.

What you now do is see what the difference is between each of the expected frequencies and each of the actual frequencies in each cell, by subtracting one from the other. This gives Figure 8.6. For clarity, the other cells have been removed.

There's now another bit of calculation, reminiscent of pulling your partner's moustache. For each of the cells in Figure 8.6, you square the number in the cell (to turn the negative numbers into positive ones), and divide the result by the number that you expected to find in that cell (from Figure 8.5), to give a relative difference. The full reasons for this are technical, and we'll considerately skip over the details; they can be tracked down fairly easily in standard stats books, if you feel the need. That gives us the numbers in Figure 8.7.

	Square pot	Oval pot	Round pot	Σ
Red counters	35.12	4.39	20.49	60
Green counters	60.88	7.61	35.51	104
Σ	96	12	56	164

Figure 8.5 Counter distributions: expected frequencies

	Square pot	Oval pot	Round pot
Red counters	16–35.12= –19.12	8–4.39 = 3.61	36–20.49 = 15.51
Green counters	80–60.88 = 19.12	4–7.61 = –3.61	20–35.51 = –15.51

Figure 8.6 Observed values minus expected values

	Square pot	Oval pot	Round pot
Red counters	(-19.12)² = 365.65 ÷35.12 = **10.41**	(3.61)² = 13.03 ÷4.39 = **2.97**	(15.51)² = 240.63 ÷20.49 = **11.74**
Green counters	(19.12)² = 365.65 ÷60.88 = **6.00**	(-3.61)² = 13.03 ÷7.61 = **1.71**	(15.51)² = 240.63 ÷35.51 = **6.78**

Figure 8.7 Squared and divided values

The penultimate step is to add these numbers up, as follows:

        10.41
         2.97
        11.74
         6.01
         1.71
         6.78
        ――――
Σ = 39.62

That's the last bit of calculation which involves these numbers. There's one more small calculation left to do, and then you can look up your result in the table. That small calculation involves subtracting 1 from the number of types of pot, giving us a value of 2, and subtracting 1 from the number of colours of counter, giving us a value of 1, and then multiplying these two values together, giving us a value of $2 \times 1 = 2$. Why do you need to do this? This involves what is known as **degrees of freedom**, a name which has inspired numerous wry thoughts among students on introductory statistics courses. In brief, it involves how many cells of a table you need to know before you can work out the values in the remaining cells. In this example, we had three pot shapes and two counter colours, giving six combinations. Once you know the values for two of the six combinations, you can work out what the values in the remaining cells have to be.

With these numbers, you can now turn to the table, and look up your results. Statistical tables are a bit like bus timetables: they look intimidating at

df	0.10	0.05	0.01	0.001
2	4.61	5.99	9.21	13.82

Figure 8.8 Part of a significance table

first sight, but they're not that bad if you work through them systematically. They also save you from a great deal of tedious calculation, and the statistical equivalent of standing in the rain for a long time because you don't know when the next bus is coming, so they're worth befriending.

In the case of the relevant table for these numbers, the first column of the table shows the numbers of degrees of freedom that each row of the table deals with, abbreviated to *df*. You run your finger down this column to the appropriate number – in this case, 2 degrees of freedom. Next, you look along this row, looking for a number close to the one that you obtained after summing all of your final totals. In this case, the number that emerged after summing all the final totals was 39.62. The relevant bit of the table is shown in Figure 8.8 (the rows above and below the relevant one have been deleted, for clarity).

The nearest number to this in the table entry for two degrees of freedom is in the last column, namely 13.82. Each column of the table shows the value needed to reach a given level of chance; for instance, if your value was 12.64, then the likelihood of this occurring by chance would be somewhere between 0.01 (one chance in a hundred) and 0.001 (one chance in a thousand). Since the value of 39.62 is well beyond the value needed to reach the 'one in a thousand' level, then the odds against these tiddlywinks scores being due just to chance are more remote than one chance in a thousand. It's therefore pretty safe to assume that there's some non-random process going on. There's a general (though not universal) convention that a result at the 'one in a thousand' level is described as 'very highly significant' statistically, which usually brings a feeling that all your number crunching was worthwhile. It also means that other researchers are likely to treat your finding as meriting closer attention and perhaps follow-up research.

You can therefore conclude that there is probably a non-random process going on – you may have been playing against an incognito tiddlywinks champion without realising it. Just what precisely that non-random process is, is another question: it's possible to imagine all sorts of scenarios, such as an incognito champion who is trying to be kind to you by deliberately missing the target pot some of the time. A disproportionate number of green counters went into the square pot, and a disproportionate number of red counters went into the round pot – does that indicate that perhaps both of you were making systematic mistakes with your tiddlywinking technique? Research findings often produce a new set of questions, and the tiddlywinks case is no exception. We'll return to the theme of multiple questions in later examples.

Some closing thoughts

After the gruelling detail of the worked example, it's a good idea to take a couple of steps back, and look at the big picture. If you're dealing with nominal categories, then the best information you can get from your data is simply the number of items which fall into each category. You can test how far these numbers diverge from what you'd expect via random chance, and you can calculate how likely it is that a given amount of divergence is the result of chance.

Tests of this sort allow to you assess whether there's a non-random tendency for some things to fall into a particular category disproportionately often. In the social sciences, this can map quite neatly onto questions such as whether a particular social group is disproportionately under- or over-represented in a particular category, such as industrial cleaner or Cabinet minister. In the life sciences, it can map quite neatly onto questions such as whether there's a disproportionate number of a particular type of insect in a given grid square. However, if you're only using nominal categories, then you're limited in what you can do. In the tiddlywinks example, for instance, the counters are either in a given pot or they're not; you can't differentiate between a counter that only just manages to get into the pot and a counter that lands beautifully on target in the centre of the pot. There are obvious advantages in being able to make distinctions of this sort, and that's something we'll return to later.

The concepts underlying non-parametric tests are fairly simple, and the arithmetic involved in working them out is not particularly taxing; you can work the results out for a typical study in a few minutes with a calculator. Most beginners, though, are likely to harbour a lurking unease about the risk of making some large and embarrassing mistake in the calculation, and will feel tempted to use a computer-based stats package instead. That's a perfectly sensible thing to do, but if you go down that route, it's highly advisable to make sure that you learn how to use the package properly, otherwise you'll simply veer from the whirlpool of wrong calculation into the monster of choosing the wrong option on the menu.

There are various tried and tested ways of learning to use the package properly. One is to go on a course; another is to ask a knowledgeable friend for help; if all else fails, you can try reading the manual (though many readers privately suspect that the manual is simply the manufacturer's opinion on how the package should be used, to paraphrase an American philosopher of everyday life). One trick of the trade which can help is to have a stats book with you when you first use a package. You can then enter the figures from a worked example in the book into the package, and see whether you end up with the same result as in the book. If the answer is very different, then you have probably done something wrong with the package, and some further exploration is needed.

That almost concludes this chapter, apart from one closing note. There's a long-established literary convention in which a true identity is exposed in the final scene; I've drawn on that convention in this chapter, and the closing note is to confirm what some readers may have already suspected, namely that the statistical test used in our worked example is technically known as a ***complex chi-squared***. I've used the most complex variety to make the point that it's not terribly complex, and that, as you might suspect from the name, the other tests in this family are simpler.

Meeting the family

Chi-squared is one of the most widely used non-parametric tests, and comes in various forms, depending on questions such as how many categories are involved; it's generally used for nominal data (i.e. categories). If you're dealing with simple binary 'either/or' values (e.g. the extreme sports club earlier in this chapter, with 'male' versus 'female') then it's usually possible to look up the probability of a given distribution directly from a table of binomial values, without having to do any intermediate calculation – the table will tell you how likely it is that you'd get, say, 18 out of 20 cases in the same category just by chance.

There are other non-parametric tests which can be used with numeric data, such as the ***Wilcoxon test*** and the ***Mann–Whitney test***; the choice between these is affected by the number of experimental conditions involved and by whether you're using a within-subject or between-subjects design. As you might guess, much could be said about this issue, and already has been, but not by us, because life is short and the word count is tight. That's it for non-parametric stats; we'll now move on to correlations.

9

Correlations

> *He did not look capable of any pleasant emotion, yet he had both blushed and simpered when Stephen . . . had cried, 'Not the illustrious Dr Juan Ramis, the author of the* Specimen Animalium?'
>
> (*Master and Commander*, p. 370)

An ancient piece of engineering wisdom advises novices to measure with a micrometer, mark with a grease pencil and cut with an axe. The example of the incognito tiddlywinks champion in the previous chapter illustrates this advice, by highlighting the loss of detail involved in registering only whether a counter went into a pot or not, without using any finer-grained information about how close the counter landed to the centre of the target. This chapter moves into more refined forms of measurement, using correlations to demonstrate the underlying concepts.

The underlying idea of a correlation is pretty simple: as one variable changes in size, so another variable tends to change with it. Sometimes both variables change in the same direction as each other (both get bigger, or both get smaller, together), in which cases the correlation is described as a positive correlation; sometimes, they change in opposite directions (one gets bigger while the other gets smaller) in which case it's known as a negative correlation. So far, so straightforward. Some correlations are linear: if you plot the two variables against each other on a scattergram, then they form a straight line. Other correlations aren't: for instance, the two variables plotted on a scattergram might produce a J-shaped line. As you might expect, there are different tests for different shapes of correlation. That's the basic idea. The next question is how to translate this idea into something that you can measure. We'll begin with a simple example. Figures 9.1–9.3 show varying amounts of correlation.

There is no clear pattern in the two sets of numbers in Figure 9.1. Sometimes a high value for variable *A* is paired with a high value for variable *B* (as with 9 and 8); sometimes a high value for *A* is paired with a low value for *B* (as with 7 and 2).

In Figure 9.2, the values for variable *A* are closely matched by the values for variable *C*, producing a strong positive correlation.

An innocent soul, faced with Figure 9.3, might be tempted to think that you could work out correlations by simple division; for instance, if you divide the value for variable *D* by 1000, you get a result which is almost exactly the same as the value for variable *A*. A less innocent soul, tempered by its journey through the chapter on measurement theory, would be more wary, and rightly so. Dividing one thing by another is all well and good if both of them are real, proper numbers of the ratio variety (i.e. ones measured on a scale with even intervals and a zero). If they're not, you might be perpetrating the equivalent of dividing your house number by your year of birth, and producing an elaborate monument to innumerate folly.

So, what can you do with correlations? You can show how strongly two variables are correlated with each other. If they're not correlated, that can tell

Variable *A*	6	4	3	8	7	9	2
Variable *B*	3	8	5	6	2	8	4

Figure 9.1 Weakly correlated numbers

Variable *A*	6	4	3	8	7	9	2
Variable *C*	5	3	1	8	5	9	4

Figure 9.2 Highly correlated numbers

Variable *A*	6	4	3	8	7	9	2
Variable *D*	6000	3999	3001	8000	7001	9000	2001

Figure 9.3 Very highly correlated numbers

you something interesting, particularly if you had prior reasons to expect them to be correlated (for instance, if you found no correlation between how much training a teacher had received and how good that teacher was at their job). If they are correlated, the knowledge that they're correlated is a start, but it doesn't tell you why that correlation occurred – the first variable might be causing the second, or the second might be causing the first, or both of them might be being caused by a third variable which you'd missed, or the correlation might just be due to chance.

How do you do correlation tests? Most people will choose the appropriate type of test for the type of measurement they've used and for the shape of correlation on a scattergram of the data, then bang the results into a stats package, which will tell them the strength of correlation between their variables on a scale from −1 (perfect negative correlation) to +1 (perfect positive correlation). If you're using an appropriate form of measurement and of research design, then the test might also tell you how likely it is that the correlation is due to chance.

That's fairly simple, but ending the chapter at this point would make it a bit short, and some readers might be eager for some technical details, so they're included below.

How do you calculate correlations? Two technical bits

The first main answer involves a solid, simple method which is the statistical equivalent of using duct tape; as you might suspect, this is the one you use if you're dealing with numbers which aren't ratio measurements. The other main answer involves a sophisticated method which uses an impressive-looking formula. If you translate that formula into ordinary English, it turns out to mean 'do this simple calculation lots of times and then press the "square root" button on your calculator', which doesn't have quite the same feel of eldritch dread. This second method is the one you use if you have numbers which involve measurements of at least the interval type and which are also normally distributed (or at least approximately so) – the sort of numbers which are so respectable that they could walk unchallenged into the Member's Area at Ascot if they were human. We'll do the simple one first.

The simple method: a slightly technical bit

The simple method starts off by translating all your numbers into the same measurement type, so you can compare like with like. You do this by translating them into an ordinal scale, which means ranking them from first to last. So, for the numbers in Figure 9.2, we get the results shown in Figure 9.4. We've inserted some subject numbers to make it clearer what's going on. We've used bland variable names, *A* and *C*, to make the point that you might be choosing to test correlations between just some of the variables that you've measured in your study; there's also the consideration that some readers might feel like some blandness after the excitement of the tiddlywinks case.

Some points of clarification: we've italicised the ranked values in Figure 9.4 for clarity, so they don't get confused with the original values. Also, two of the values for variable *C* were the same, and the convention in such cases is to give them the same rank value in the way we've shown. The two numbers involved (both a score of 5) need to share ranks 3 and 4 between them, and that's done by giving them both the (mean) ranking of 3.5, and continuing from there with the next number being ranked 5.

The second step is to calculate the difference between each pair of ranks, by subtracting one from the other. Why? Because if the two sets of variables are strongly positively correlated, then there won't be much difference between the rankings – a high ranking on one variable will usually be accompanied by a high ranking on the other, and so on. If they're strongly negatively correlated, then there will be big differences between the rankings, since a high ranking on one variable will usually be accompanied by a low ranking on the other. If there's no correlation between the two sets of variables, there will be a roughly even mixture of large and small differences in rankings, which will in effect cancel each other out. (It's unwise to ask awkward questions about whether it's mathematically legitimate to subtract ranks from each other, unless you really fancy a long and very technical answer, or possibly a short and impolite one, depending on whom you ask and how you phrase the question.) That gives us Figure 9.5. The difference is indicated by the symbol *d* (a simple mnemonic is to think of it as standing for 'difference').

The third step is the old favourite of squaring one batch of numbers

Subject no.	s1	s2	s3	s4	s5	s6	s7
Variable *A*	6	4	3	8	7	9	2
Ranks *A*	*4*	*5*	*6*	*2*	*3*	*1*	*7*
Variable *C*	5	3	1	8	5	9	4
Ranks *C*	*3.5*	*6*	*7*	*2*	*3.5*	*1*	*5*

Figure 9.4 Data from Figure 9.2, with ranks added

Subject no.	s1	s2	s3	s4	s5	s6	s7
Ranks A	4	5	6	2	3	1	7
Ranks C	3.5	6	7	2	3.5	1	5
d	0.5	1	1	0	0.5	0	2

Figure 9.5 Differences between rankings

Subject no.	s1	s2	s3	s4	s5	s6	s7
Ranks A	4	5	6	2	3	1	7
Ranks C	3.5	6	7	2	3.5	1	5
d	+0.5	1	1	0	−0.5	0	2
d^2	0.25	1	1	0	0.25	0	4

Figure 9.6 Differences and squared differences between rankings

(i.e. multiplying each one by itself) for the usual reasons of converting everything to a positive number, emphasising any unusually high numbers so you reach a conservative figure rather than a wildly hopeful one, and so forth. That gives you the results in Figure 9.6.

The next couple of steps involve adding up all the individual results for d^2 so that you can see how much difference there is overall; this produces a number that you can look up in a table which someone else has prepared earlier. You do it like this.

First you add up the individual values for d^2. This gives you

$$\Sigma d^2 = 0.25 + 1 + 1 + 0 + 0 + 0.25 + 0 + 4 = 6.5.$$

Next, you allow for the number of subjects that were involved in making up this score – the more subjects you have, the bigger the score is likely to be, so you need to take that into account. You do this by counting the number of subjects ($n = 7$), and then doing some simple calculations, as follows.

First, multiply your Σd^2 result (i.e. 6.5) by 6. (The reasons for the number 6 are too technical to cover here.) This gives you a total of 39.

Second, square the number of your subjects, and subtract 1 from the result. This gives you $49 - 1 = 48$.

Third, multiply the number you've just calculated (i.e. 48) by your number of subjects (i.e. 7). This gives you a total of 336, which is the number that you need to include in your calculations to allow for how many subjects you have; we now return to the main process, where we'll apply the allowance.

The antepenultimate step is to divide your total of 39 (from the bit where you multiplied Σd^2 by 6) by your total of 336 (from the bit where you squared the number of subjects, subtracted 1, and multiplied the result by the number of subjects). This step is the one which actually applies the allowance for the number of subjects in your sample; it gives you a total of $39/336 = 0.116071$.

The penultimate step is to calculate the value for subtracting that last total from 1. This gives you $1 - 0.116071 = 0.883929$. Why subtract the last total from 1? This is a common device in statistics, and is often useful for translating a number into a more convenient format. 'More convenient' can mean various things, such as 'smaller' or 'allowing you to add things together instead of having to multiply them'. The precise reasons in *this* case are well described in the standard texts, if you feel an ardent desire to get into the minutiae; we will, however, return to the main story.

This final value is known as *rho*, pronounced like 'roe'. The highest value you can get for rho is 1; the lowest is −1. A value of 1 indicates perfect positive correlation; a value of −1 indicates perfect negative correlation; a value of 0 indicates no correlation. The value of 0.883929 is quite near to 1, so it's a very high correlation, which means that you may well have found an effect worth bothering with.

The final step is to look up your *rho* value in the relevant table, to find out its level of statistical significance. The relevant line of that table shows the values needed to attain statistical significance with $n = 7$ subjects (Figure 9.7). The value of 0.883929 which we have just calculated comes between the values of 0.786 and 0.893 listed in the table, so its statistical significance is somewhere between the two corresponding probability values of 0.05 and 0.02; in other words, the likelihood of this result being due to chance is somewhere between one chance in 20 and one chance in a 50. In statistical language, this result is statistically significant at the 0.05 level. You can therefore treat these results as probably being the result of an effect, rather than random chance.

Being a forgiving and tolerant method, this way of calculating correlations is pretty popular. It's particularly useful for things like calculating correlations

n	0.10	0.05	0.02	0.01
7	0.714	0.786	0.893	0.929

Figure 9.7 Part of a significance table

from Likert-style scales, where you ask your respondents to rate something on a scale of 1 to 7 (or whatever set of numbers you have happened to choose). You could use this method to calculate, for instance, whether someone's ratings of the desirability of assorted products are correlated with their ratings of the likely cost of those products. When this method was first developed, large numbers of researchers rushed out to apply it to more or less everything in sight, including correlating the number of segments in earthworms with the length of the said earthworms, which is testimony to its usefulness.

The name of this test is the ***Spearman rank correlation coefficient***, rather than something humbler such as 'the simple correlation method'. A brief parenthesis: you might wonder why statistical tests have the sort of names that they do. One unkind speculation is that statisticians are no fools when it comes to naming tests after themselves (such as Spearman and his rank correlation coefficient). When you're applying for a prestigious job, you're in a much stronger position if people say: 'Gosh, are you *the* Spearman that the test is named after?' This gives you the chance to approximate a coy simper and to outshine the other candidates. Cynical people might also suspect, along similar lines, that if you include a description of what the test does within its name, then (a) people will be more likely to choose it when they work through a list of prospective tests to apply to their data and (b) it gives you scope to have several tests named after yourself, rather than just one (if you called it simply 'Spearman's test', for instance). The truth, for once, is more inspiring: tests are given names by the statistical community, not by the person inventing them, so neither of these suspicions is justified. Returning to the names themselves, the last bit which often crops up in the name of a test is what you call the number that emerges from the test, such as the ***Mann–Whitney U test***, invented by Mann and Whitney, which produces a number called *U*. Some students find an unholy pleasure in being able to use tests with names such as the ***Kolmogorov–Smirnov one-sample test***; others don't.

There is a certain amount of satisfaction in being able to use the Spearman rank correlation coefficient, but that satisfaction is usually mixed with some vexation about having to translate your raw data into ordinal measurements along the way; it feels as if you're throwing away some of your hard-earned precision. It's an understandable feeling, and it tends to leave students wondering about some more powerful tests which will show more appreciation of their elegant measurements. There are indeed such tests, and we'll now have a brief encounter with one.

The test with the impressive-looking formula (a more technical bit)

This test allows you to measure correlations between two sets of variables, where both sets of numbers are interval or ratio measurements and where both sets of numbers are (approximately) normally distributed. That's a moderately exclusive beginning – it keeps out nominal and ordinal values. We'll use an example from nature to demonstrate how this method works, in the form of preferred sleeping height for adult male gorillas. Gorillas sleep in nests in trees when young, but as the males become older and heavier, the risk increases of unpleasant accidents involving branches snapping in the night, and sudden, undesired contact with the ground, so their preferred sleeping height decreases. We'll use hypothetical data, showing the age of each gorilla and the height of its nest (Figure 9.8). Readers familiar with gorilla nesting habits will notice that the figures are not wildly realistic; readers who have tried inventing highly realistic normally distributed data for gorilla ages and nest heights will understand why we're running with what we have. To make life simpler, ages are shown using decimals, such as '3.5 years', rather than years and months.

There are now five steps. Most of these steps involve calculations which are pretty simple, but which are also pretty numerous, so we'll go into the general principles but bypass the more tedious bits of calculation.

The first step involves multiplying each of the age scores by each of the nest height scores. This step makes use of your raw numbers – it doesn't translate them into some less precise format such as ordinal measurements.

The next step involves squaring each of the age scores and squaring each of the nest height scores. This is done to allow for the amount of variation within each set of scores. If you have noisy, very variable, data then you need to make more allowance for the risk of finding a correlation that's just the result of chance. It also translates all these scores into positive numbers. The results from these two steps are shown in a Figure 9.9.

The third step is to use the numbers you have just calculated, and do a further set of calculations with them, using an impressive-looking formula. I've omitted the formula and the calculations, on the grounds that (a) you can

Subject	s1	s2	s3	s4	s5	s6	s7	s8	s9	s10	s11
Age	1.2	6.2	3.5	9.1	8.6	3.2	4.8	2.4	5.3	6.3	5.1
Nest height	8.4	3.1	6.4	1.2	2.3	6.6	5.4	7.1	4.7	3.6	4.8

Figure 9.8 Gorilla ages and nest heights

Subject	Age (A)	Height (H)	A × H	A²	H²
s1	1.2	8.4	10.08	1.44	70.56
s2	6.2	3.1	19.22	38.44	9.61
s3	3.5	6.4	22.4	12.25	40.96
s4	9.1	1.2	10.92	82.81	1.44
s5	8.6	2.3	19.78	73.96	5.29
s6	3.2	6.6	21.12	10.24	43.56
s7	4.8	5.4	25.92	23.04	29.16
s8	2.4	7.1	17.04	5.76	50.41
s9	5.3	4.7	24.91	28.09	22.09
s10	6.3	3.6	22.68	39.69	12.96
s11	5.1	4.8	24.48	26.01	23.04
Total	**55.7**	**53.6**	**218.55**	**341.73**	**309.08**
Square	**3102.49**	**2872.96**	**47764.10**	**116779.39**	**95530.45**

Figure 9.9 Gorilla ages and nest heights, with some calculations

find them easily in any stats book if you really want them, and (b) few readers will be much inclined to cope with them at this stage. Each calculation is simple, but there are a lot of them. At the end of these calculations, you emerge with a number: in this case, it's -0.98861.

What's going on in this formula is that you're working out the amount of difference between each measurement and its pair on the other variable (i.e. the age and the nest height for each gorilla), taking into account that the data are normally distributed. Because the data are normally distributed, you can calculate very precise figures for how likely it is that a given data point will be a given distance from the mean score for that particular variable (e.g. the mean nest height). You can also calculate the corresponding likelihood for the pair on the other variable for that data point (i.e. the values for the age and the nest height), and then calculate the likelihood of both of them happening to be as far as they are from the mean. As you might imagine, this involves quite a lot of calculations, which is why you've been spared the detail.

The penultimate step is to calculate the *degrees of freedom*, on the same principle as with non-parametric statistics – that is, calculate how many values you need to know before you can deduce what the remaining values must be. In this particular example, the degrees of freedom is two less than the number of subjects: 11 subjects minus 2, giving 9. The greater the degrees of freedom, the more things there are going on in your data, and the more allowance the test needs to make for these.

The last step, as is traditional, is to go to the appropriate table, and look up the row for 9 degrees of freedom, to see where your final number belongs. When you do that, the result is very highly statistically significant, at well beyond the level of 0.001. The conclusion is that there is a very strong statistical correlation between age and nest height.

This is what the formula actually looks like:

$$r = \frac{\sum_{i=1}^{n}(A_i - \bar{A})(H_i - \bar{H})}{\sqrt{\sum_{i=1}^{n}(A_i - \bar{A})^2 \sum_{i=1}^{n}(H_i - \bar{H})^2}}$$

It involves a lot of calculations, although they're all pretty straightforward. In case you're wondering, they consist of several multiplications, a smattering of division, the odd square root, some subtraction, and the occasional episode of multiplying a number by itself a few times. The tricky part is keeping track of where you are in the process. This is where stats packages are helpful, because they do the appropriate calculations for you in the right sequence. You simply put in the numbers for your data, the software plugs the numbers into the formula, and the end product is a single number: in this example, it's −0.98861.

The formal name for this test is the **Pearson product moment correlation test**. It's named, unsurprisingly, after Pearson. Being parametric and sniffy about the sort of data that it associates with, it's a more powerful test than its non-parametric relations, and you can therefore draw more powerful conclusions from the same quantity of data.

Meet the family

There are, as you might expect, various tests of correlation which are appropriate for different purposes, such as the type of measurement you're using, whether you're dealing with normally distributed data or not, and whether the data form a straight line on a scattergram (a linear correlation) or form another shape such as a 'J' curve. Stats books normally include a table or decision tree showing which tests are appropriate for each of these situations. In addition, there are a couple of other useful concepts relating to correlations. Both our examples involved finding correlations between two variables. You might have wondered about what you could do with more than two variables. The answer is that if the data are of the appropriate form, then you can do multiple correlations, which involve working out how strong the correlation is between each of the possible permutations of variables. Because of the number of calculations involved, it's usually preferable to use a stats package for this. The good news is that this can find correlations which you might otherwise never have thought of (for instance, shoe size will probably correlate with income); the bad news is that because of the sheer number of possible permutations, at least some of these correlations are likely to be due to nothing more than chance. If you're thinking of trying this approach, then you'd be wise to talk to a statistician before formalising your research design, so that you don't end up with a pile of inscrutable grot.

Another related concept involves going beyond eyeballing when assessing the shape of a scattergram distribution. For instance, if your scattergram shows a trend which looks like a steady upwards climb, then you might be wondering whether there's a way of calculating some sort of idealised line through the middle of the data points, to show their overall tendency. The answer is that you can, and that this is known as *regression*. This can be particularly useful for a couple of purposes. One is assessing the shape of a trend more objectively than can be done by eye (useful if you have a lot of data and a lot of variance within that data). Another is finding an underlying correspondence between the variables involved (e.g. 'the value for A increases about twice as fast as the value for B'). It's also possible to do multiple regressions, which are a Good Thing, but outside our scope, so on that note we'll move on to the next topic, namely parametric statistics.

10

Parametric statistics

Experimental design and parametric statistics • Meet the family

> *The barnacle beckoned. He anticipated a short descriptive paper.*
> (*Darwin*, p. 339)

Parametric statistics are a Good Thing, thoroughly covered in numerous statistics books, and so respectable that they could settle in Edinburgh without raising any eyebrows. They also involve calculations which, though individually simple, are numerous to the point of tedium. In addition, they are usually used in conjunction with well-established formal experimental designs. Taken together, these attributes provide only limited raw material for inventive description, but so it goes, sometimes.

In this chapter, we will cover the main concepts underlying how parametric statistics are used. There is little about the minutiae of the calculations, but a moderate amount about experimental design and its intimate association with parametric tests.

First, though, there's a simple question to answer. Parametric statistics are used on data that are normally distributed (or approximately so); how, though, can a would-be user tell whether or not their data are normally distributed? There are two simple answers. The first is that if you're a humble student, you can probably get away with just doing a histogram of the data, and seeing whether it looks like the normal distributions that you've seen in books. (It would, however, be wise to check with your supervisor whether this is enough in your discipline.) The second is that if you're in a discipline which is sniffy about such things, there are statistical tests which will tell you whether or not your data form a normal distribution. (Readers with a taste for irony might like to know that these tests are based on non-parametric statistics.)

Once you have done this, the core underlying concept is a simple one. If you know that something is normally distributed throughout a population (e.g. foot sizes among adult males), then you can tell how likely it is that you will get a particular set of values for the samples that you happen to take from within that population. For instance, if the sample of adult males you collected in Luton contains higher values for foot sizes than the sample of adult males from Scunthorpe, you can calculate how likely it is that these differences are due to simple random chance (i.e. that there's actually no systematic difference in foot sizes between Luton adult males and Scunthorpe adult males – that you just happen to have ended up with more big-footed individuals in your Luton sample than in your Scunthorpe sample). Because the normal distribution is so specifically defined, this means that you can calculate values using a smaller sample size than would have been the case with a non-normal distribution. In this sense, the underlying concept is the same for both parametric and non-parametric tests: you're just seeing how likely it is that your findings are due to nothing more than chance.

The next step is to decide which variety of parametric statistics you want to use, and that takes us into the purposes for which they are used, which in turn takes us into the issue of experimental design. The customary way of doing this is via worthy descriptions of experiments manipulating condition A and condition B; by way of giving the hard-worked A and B a rest, we'll instead tackle the principles via the example of competitive sport.

Experimental design and parametric statistics

Back in the Past, before improving literature had been invented, the dominant figures in heroic societies used various methods for passing the time. One of these was competition of various forms. The disastrous Cattle Raid of Cooley began with Conchobar and Medhbh competitively boasting about the number of goods that they owned; the *Iliad* ends with descriptions of funeral games. Few of these dominant figures achieved fame for being a good loser, and there were numerous ways in which they could wriggle out of a situation which looked like a potential loss. Much the same applies today.

Imagine, for instance, that you are on a field trip to a particularly bleak, windswept bit of shoreline, and that your supervisor has given you the task of measuring movement rates in limpets. Limpets, like Barbara Cartland, suffer many cruel remarks from unkind people, and are more interesting than is generally realised; for instance, some limpets are territorial, engaging in titanic struggles for control of favoured grazing spots, whereas others are nomadic, cruising from one stretch of rock to another like underwater vegetarian Hell's Angels without motorbikes. That said, they're still not the most thrilling thing in the world, especially when the windchill is starting to bite and you're even starting to think of the hostel as comparatively warm. Imagine, then, that you and a fellow-student decide to relieve the monotony by trying two different methods of increasing limpet speed, with the loser having to buy cocoa for the winner when you finally get back to the hostel. You opt for warming the limpets gently to increase their metabolic rate; your opponent opts for feeding them some particularly tasty algae to boost their energy reserves. You choose your teams; you set up the track; you prepare the limpets, and watch them rush down the home straight; your limpets lose comprehensively. What face-saving excuses can you offer?

There are plenty. You could point out that your opponent's limpets were racing along a smooth bit of the rock, unlike your bit, which featured a lot of obstructive barnacles. You might also point out that the bit of rock that your limpets had to race along was steeper than the bit of rock that your opponent's limpets had. There's also the counter-argument that limpets seldom get a chance to race in ideal conditions, so it might be more realistic to measure their performance on a rough track. In summary, if you want to know which team was really the better team, you'd need to race them in conditions which give a fair comparison, and you'd need to ask several questions, not just one. This takes us out of competitive sport and into the calmer waters of experimental design and parametric statistics.

The case of the unequivalent limpets can be represented as a set of four possibilities. The races can be run in four combinations:

- pre-warmed, good track;
- pre-warmed, bad track;
- pre-fed, good track;
- pre-fed, bad track.

What you can therefore do is get the unfortunate limpets to race under each of these four conditions, and then see who has the best score overall. That's feasible if all the limpets are able to run all four races, but in reality there's a fair chance that one of them will tear a muscle or have a previous engagement for at least one race, so you'll need to find some way of working out what their score would have been, on the basis of their scores in the races which they did run. If that happens, some stats tests can make allowances for the missing values, but others can't; we'll leave that issue to one side for the moment.

Another issue in arranging a fair race takes us back to the concepts of between-subjects and within-subject designs. If you have different limpets running each of the four races, then there's a chance that the set of limpets running one race might just happen to be better or worse than the other sets of limpets. Suppose, for instance, that you just happen to have a set of brilliant limpets running the 'pre-fed, bad track' race, and talent-free amateurs running the others; then you'd probably end up with a faster set of scores from the brilliant limpets, even though that race would be over worse terrain. There would be obvious advantages in having the same limpets run each course, if you could manage it, because that would remove the risk of having one group which happened to perform differently from the others, as an added complicating factor. This is why most researchers use within-subject (i.e. 'same athlete') designs if they can.

Counterbalancing is another relevant issue at this point. If your limpets have to do the bad track on the first test, then they're likely to have sore muscles and to run slower in the next trial than they would have done otherwise. The sensible thing is therefore to balance out the sequence in which the limpets have to run each test, so that some of them do the bad track followed by the good track, and others do the good track followed by the bad track. The more types of track that are involved, the more combinations you need to allow for. If you're of a tidy disposition, you can draw this up as a systematic table showing which combinations are possible, and which of your limpets is doing which combination.

As if these assorted complications are not enough, there's also the consideration that limpets might vary from day to day, like people. Sometimes you wake feeling fresh and lively; sometimes you don't. It's likely that within each group of limpets on any given day, some will be having a better day than usual, and running that little bit faster. If you happen to have a group of limpets all of whom happen by chance to be having a good day for different reasons during the same race, then that will produce a faster set of results for that type of race, just by random chance.

The result of allowing for all of these variables is that you have an elegant experimental design even before you start using the stats. The good side of this is that the design gives you a clear set of questions, which are answered systematically by the statistics. This in turn makes it much easier to understand what the statistics are achieving, regardless of how they get there.

In the case of the unequivalent limpets, we end up with the following set of possible questions:

- How much variation is there in each limpet's performance when running the same track on different occasions?
- How much variation is there between the scores for each of the four permutations of preparation regime and track type?
- How much variation is there between the preparation regimes, once you've allowed for different track types?
- How much variation is there between the good track and the bad track, once you've allowed for preparation regime?
- If we use a between-groups design, with different limpets doing each track, then we also need to ask how much variation is due to variations between groups.

What now happens is that the statistics package calculates the values for each of these sources of variation. For example, it works out the amount of variability within a single limpet's scores, and the amount of variability within a group's scores; it also works out the amount of difference between the collected scores for each track, and compares that difference with the amount of variability that you get within each group and within each subject. So, for example, if a particular limpet produces consistently low scores on the bad track, and consistently high scores on the good track, regardless of preparation regime, then the main likely cause for the differences in scores is the tracks rather than the preparation regime.

One last consideration when you use parametric statistics is the number of degrees of freedom involved. In brief, the more things you're varying in your experimental design, the more allowances the software needs to make in its calculations. The degrees of freedom relate to how many things the software needs to know about your results before it can extrapolate the remaining things from what it already knows. The formulae that go with each test will tell you how to calculate the degrees of freedom for your particular case. This usually involves subtracting a number from your number of subjects (n) – for instance, $n - 1$.

What you get from all this is an impressive-looking output from the stats package (we're assuming that you won't want to do the calculations in person). The details will vary depending on the test, but they will usually include some or more of the following.

- A figure for the amount of variance due to your first variable (in this case, whether you pre-warm or pre-feed the limpets).
- A figure for the amount of variance due to your second variable (in this case, whether the track is good or bad).
- A figure for the interaction of the two variables. This is because each of the variables may be individually innocuous, but a particular combination of variables may produce a disproportionate result. For instance, holding a conversation is fairly simple, though mildly surreal, while you are either patting your head or rubbing your stomach, but attempting to hold a conversation while doing both simultaneously is a different proposition.
- More or less last, there will be a figure for 'error variance'. This relates to the amount of chance variation that is floating around, not attributable to any of the variables you have used in your design (in essence, a figure for the size of the 'happening to have a bad day or good day' effect). Nervous students might be glad to hear that it's not a measure of how many things they got wrong. There will also be a figure for the total variance, which is the sum of the figures above.

As is customary with inferential statistics, the test will also give you a probability value for your findings, which may not be immediately obvious, since it will be accompanied by figures for all the other things just mentioned.

Here is an example; the figures for limpet speeds in Figure 10.1 are hypothetical, as is customary, which saves us from some bleak hours at the seaside. For brevity, we'll skip over the details of the formulae involved in analysing these; we'll assume instead that you will feed them into a stats package such as

Group	Good track	Bad track
Pre-warmed	20.50	30.50
Pre-warmed	55.00	65.00
Pre-warmed	20.00	22.00
Pre-warmed	22.00	25.00
Pre-warmed	30.00	29.00
Pre-warmed	25.00	27.00
Pre-warmed	50.00	60.00
Pre-warmed	29.00	35.00
Pre-warmed	33.00	37.00
Pre-warmed	19.00	21.00
Pre-fed	19.25	25.00
Pre-fed	25.00	27.00
Pre-fed	29.00	35.00
Pre-fed	17.00	19.00
Pre-fed	25.00	29.00
Pre-fed	33.00	37.00
Pre-fed	25.00	25.00
Pre-fed	18.00	20.00
Pre-fed	40.00	45.00
Pre-fed	22.00	26.00

Figure 10.1 Raw data for limpet performance

Minitab or SPSS. What happens when you do this? What happens is that you get lots and lots of analyses. They'll include (depending on the package you use, and the options you select) within-subjects factors, between-subjects factors, and a summary of the descriptive statistics for your data, by way of an appetiser. They'll also include assorted figures for the actual inferential statistics, such as **Pillai's trace, Wilks' lambda, Hotelling's trace** and **Roy's largest root** (and no, none of these names is fictitious, which must prove something about the effects on the human psyche of prolonged exposure to statistics, at least as regards naming of tests). Once you've waded through all that lot, not forgetting **Mauchler's test of sphericity** (which is also not fictitious) you'll come to a set of tables which show results for within-subjects effects, another set which show results for within-subjects contrasts, and a third set which show results for between-subjects effects. They'll include columns showing values for things like **Type III sum of squares** and **partial eta squared** (again, real, not fictitious). By this stage, if this is your first exposure to stats packages, you'll probably be feeling a bit overwhelmed. One column, though, might catch your attention; with a name along the lines of 'Sig.' and values which look like *p* values, you might correctly guess that it contains the statistical significance values for your results. There are also figures for the strength of the effect.

In case the suspense is too much for you, we'll cut to the short answer, which is that the track makes an astoundingly significant difference to the limpets' performance, but that there's no significant difference between the pre-warmed and the pre-fed limpets, or between the groups of limpets involved. That being so, why did the package give you such a huge amount of information in response to a simple question? The answer is that the original question actually wasn't simple; it was actually a complex set of questions, once you work through all the implications and permutations of what you initially wanted to know.

Because parametric statistics take so many things into account, and give you numbers for the relative amount of effect they have on the final probability value, they allow you to answer a lot of questions at once. In this case, for instance, they would allow you to give figures for the relative effects of each preparation regime on limpet speeds, and to tell whether these differences were at a level beyond chance. They also give you comparative figures for the two different types of track, and for interactions between preparation regime and track type (e.g. whether pre-warming raises performance on a smooth track but lowers performance on a rough track). Even an apparently simple question involving a couple of variables will unpack into a large number of component questions, and these will require a large number of answers.

Because parametric tests give you figures for the effects of the variables involved, they lend themselves nicely to being combined with formal experimental designs in which you decide which variables you want to investigate, and then manipulate them systematically. This is why the formal experimental design combined with parametric statistics is often held up as the most elegant form of research design – you can reduce the problem to a tightly defined set of variables, and then show with elegant minimalism what effect each variable has. It's a nice feeling, if your research question is of a form which allows you to use this approach.

That's the end of this description of basic parametric statistics. Some readers might at this point be wondering hopefully whether it's also the end of everything there is to know about statistics; others, trying to solve research questions of a type not described so far, might be wondering dejectedly whether there is no hope left. The answer is that there's a bit more to cover, in the form of multidimensional statistics, which can be very useful if you're dealing with large numbers of variables and trying to find some underlying patterns in them. They are the topic of the next chapter, which is the last chapter about types of statistical test. On that note, we'll proceed to the 'meet the family' subsection about types of parametric tests.

Meet the family

If you're dealing with a simple research design involving only one variable, then you can use various parametric tests, such as the *t test* and the ***one-way ANOVA*** (ANalysis Of VAriance). As usual, the choice is affected by issues such as whether you're using a within-subject or between-subjects design, and how many experimental conditions you're using. If you're dealing with two or more variables, then the usual choice is some form of ***two-way ANOVA***. As you might have guessed, I do not propose to go into detail about this, and will instead repeat the usual advice that the wisest strategy is to discuss your intentions with someone knowledgeable before firming up your research design. That having been said, we will move on to our next topic, multidimensional statistics.

11

Multidimensional statistics

The simple bit about the underlying concepts • The sophisticated bit • The bit about underlying assumptions • Some technical terms and further thoughts • Beyond statistics: approaches related and complementary to multidimensional statistics

> *He had been thinking too much about the vague regions which his formulae told him must lie beyond the three dimensions we know . . .*
>
> *(The Dreams in the Witch-House, p. 309)*

In the chapter about correlations, I mentioned that it was possible to do multiple correlations, to see how much each variable correlated with each of the other variables. Readers of a thoughtful disposition might have wondered about the implications of multiple correlations, and rightly so. For instance, suppose that you were looking at correlations between variables in a study of obesity among middle-aged males, with those males ranging in shape from pretty skinny to very obese. You'd probably find a correlation between height and body weight, with tall men tending to be heavier than short men, though it wouldn't be a very strong correlation, since men of the same height could be anywhere between very skinny and very obese. You'd almost certainly also find correlations between assorted girth measurements and weight – for instance, chest measurement, waist measurement, hip measurement, upper thigh and upper arm measurement would probably all correlate strongly with each other and also correlate with weight.

At this point, various thoughts might occur to you. You might wonder, for instance, whether there was much point in measuring chest measurement as well as waist measurement and hip measurement and the others: if they're strongly correlated, then measuring just one of them would give you a pretty good idea of what the values would be for the others. You might also start wondering just how many things you needed to know before you could predict someone's weight accurately – for instance, if you knew their height and their waist measurement, would this be all that you needed to know in order to make a good prediction? This might in turn spark some wider speculations: for example, about how many apparently complicated questions involving lots of variables can be answered by measuring just a few of those variables, since the remaining variables aren't telling you anything new. You might wonder, also, whether some statistical test with a big name has been designed to tackle problems of this sort.

If those thoughts, or ones along those lines, have been crossing your mind, then your life might be brightened by the news that it is indeed possible to do these things for at least some problems, which is what this chapter is about.

There are various tests which allow you to look for key variables in this way, such as **Principal Component Analysis** and *factor analysis*. All involve heavy-duty maths for the detailed calculations, and I won't attempt to cram the details into this book. The underlying concepts, though, are pretty simple.

The simple bit about the underlying concepts

What the tests do, in essence, is as follows. First, they see how strongly each variable is correlated with each of the other variables. Once this has been done, they attempt to identify clusters of variables. Within each cluster, the variables will all correlate fairly strongly with each other, and presumably be variants on a single theme. In the case of the potentially obese males, for example, there would be one cluster of variables which involve variants on the theme of circumference: the dimensions for the respondent's chest measurement, waist measurement, hip measurement, and so on; there would also be a second cluster of variables which involve variants on the theme of height, such as length of thigh bone, length of upper arm, etc. You might also have a third cluster involving the percentage of the individual's body mass which consisted of fat as opposed to muscle, bone or organs. You can now see which individual variables are the best predictors of weight, and also see how well each cluster of variables predicts weight.

Now comes one of the cunning bits. The cluster with the strongest correlation might, for example, allow you to predict a respondent's weight with a fair degree of accuracy. What the software can now do is, in effect, to see whether tweaking this result in light of the result from another cluster of variables will allow you to make a more accurate prediction. Once it's done that, it can then repeat the process for each of the other clusters.

So, for instance, you might find that the girth measurements give you a pretty good estimate of the respondent's weight. The height measurements on their own might not be very good predictors, but if you make a prediction based on a combination both of the girth measurements and of the height measurements as well, then the combination of the two will give you a better estimate of the respondent's weight than you'd get from either measurement on its own. So, for instance, a tall obese man will probably weigh more than a short obese man. If you now combine these variables with variables from the third cluster, you might get an even better estimate, even though the third cluster on its own might be quite a poor predictor.

What typically happens in a lot of fields is that the first cluster gives you predictions which are pretty good; the second group adds a reasonable amount to the prediction, and the third group adds a small amount. After that, the remaining groups typically don't give you much worth bothering with. At this point, the nice simple part of the explanation comes to a gentle close, and the sophisticated bit starts.

The sophisticated bit

Just as driving across London in rush hour is a simple goal involving a very large quantity of practical detail in its execution, so doing multidimensional statistics is simple in concept but not quite so simple in its assumptions and its calculations. It also involves some concepts which look deceptively familiar, but which are in fact not what they might appear. We'll start with one of the deceptively familiar-looking things, to finish the point about the various clusters' contributions to your predictions.

Tests of this sort typically produce an output which tells you what proportion of the *variance* is accounted for by each of the clusters. This looks like a percentage, but it's not a percentage of the common or garden variety, for reasons too technical to concern us. For our present purposes, we'll pretend that the figure is a real percentage, but that's just a simplifying fiction. As for what 'variance' is, that's another question to be postponed for a while; for the time being, we'll pretend that it's another term for how good your prediction is.

What you typically find if you apply multidimensional statistics to living organisms is that the first cluster of variables accounts for a high proportion of the accuracy in your prediction. In the case of predicting weight of middle-aged men, for example, the girth measurement might account for 70% of the variance. The next cluster typically accounts for a much smaller percentage – maybe 20%. The third cluster may contribute something like another 5%. The stats package will also tell you how strong an association there is between each of your original variables and each of the factors/principal components identified by the software. In the case of our hypothetical weight example, once you knew the values for an individual's girth and for the two other factors/ principal components, then you could make a pretty accurate prediction of the individual's weight from those values alone – allowing for the other variables as well wouldn't increase the accuracy much.

If you do the same for some other types of problem, then you quite often get a different pattern, where none of your clusters contributes more than about 20% of the variance, and none of your variables correlates with anything to an extent that's worth a damn. Interpretations of 'worth a damn' vary across disciplines and research areas. In some areas, a correlation of less than 0.8 is viewed with aloof disdain; in others, a correlation as high as 0.3 is viewed as a finding worthy of a journal publication. Researchers in the former areas often tend towards the opinion that researchers in the latter areas are a bunch of amateurs who don't know how to find and measure the right variables; researchers in the latter areas often tend towards the opinion that researchers in the former areas are a bunch of effete cherry-pickers who work in an easy area because they don't know how to tackle difficult problems.

This can be a particularly interesting question in areas such as social science research. A classic example is the decades-old set of vendettas relating to measures of intelligence, and to questions such as whether 'intelligence' is a single thing manifesting itself in different ways, or a bunch of separate things which have been lumped together under the same name. A sweetly innocent view might be that multidimensional statistics would be the tool allowing us to answer these questions. In reality, multidimensional statistics in this context are more like heavy spanners being picked up in a menacing manner by two opposing groups of feuding mechanics. The reasons for this take us into some of the underlying assumptions on which the various tests are based.

The bit about underlying assumptions

The simple bit above included a casual mention that the test would 'identify clusters of variables'. That's fairly similar to saying that your next task is to work out the seating plan for a wedding and subsequent dinner: an apparently innocent task heavy with potential for unexpected disaster. Some of the seating decisions are simple: for instance, the bride's brother is a straightforward case of a clear relative of the bride. Other relationships are simple and distant – second cousins and the like. A large number, though, are awkward. What about someone who's a stepbrother of the groom and a cousin of the bride? Or someone who's a close friend of both the bride and groom? What about the two brothers of the bride who haven't been on speaking terms for ten years, or the uncle who needs to be kept away from the drink?

It's just the same when you start deciding how to put variables together into clusters. There are lots of sensible ways to do it, which will usually agree on the first couple of easy decisions, and will then disagree completely with each other when it comes to the remaining decisions about the majority of the variables. In the case of the great debate about intelligence, for instance, one set of assumptions produces clusterings which suggest that intelligence is a single underlying entity; another set of equally valid assumptions, however, produces clusterings which suggest that intelligence is a batch of separate entities.

The situation isn't helped much by the consideration that most things in life correlate with most other things to at least some extent, as a result of reasons some distance removed. If you drag variables through multidimensional statistics, you can end up finding clusters of variables whose connections to each other are tenuous at best. For example, as year follows year through the calendar, the Atlantic Ocean will broaden due to continental drift; cumulative sales for Barbara Cartland novels will climb; California redwood trees will produce further sets of growth rings. During those same years, the world price of copper will wander up and down, probably mirrored by house prices in Edinburgh, which in turn will probably be mirrored by champagne sales in Greater Manchester. Within each of these clusters, the variables will correlate strongly with each other, but variables from one cluster won't correlate strongly with variables from the other cluster. Does this mean that the Atlantic Ocean, Barbara Cartland's novels and California redwoods form part of some tightly knit group of things, and that you might have discovered some previously unsuspected form of morphic resonance? What it actually means is that many things in the universe get steadily bigger with time; those things don't necessarily have anything else in common with each other. Similarly, other things in the human world are affected by the state of the economy, but have little else in common with each other. In the Atlantic/Cartland/redwoods example, it's pretty obvious that the correlations are by-products of something else (i.e. the passage of time). If, however, you'd found equally strong correlations involving scores on several different psychological tests, you could easily be tempted to assume that you'd discovered a real underlying common factor based on a real causal connection. How can you tell which of these cases applies to your data? That's something that stats alone can't normally answer; that's where your analysis of the literature and of the underlying causal mechanisms should be able to throw some light. (So would a formal experiment, in some cases – for instance, you could spend a large chunk of your research budget buying huge quantities of champagne in Greater Manchester, to see whether that affected world copper prices and Edinburgh house prices.) As usual, the statistics are a tool to be used in conjunction with your overall research framework.

Some technical terms and further thoughts

Most of the terms used above have technical equivalents with more professional credibility. A slightly complicating issue is that the same basic concept may be defined in two subtly but importantly different ways by two rival approaches. The underlying clusters are usually called 'factors', which is why I have studiously avoided the word 'factor' throughout the rest of this book.

Multidimensional stats are the statistical equivalent of a cannon in the fifteenth century: a weapon which can bring low an enemy or a research problem quite spectacularly, if it doesn't happen to blow up and mangle you instead. If some pompous individual is vapouring on about how a particular question involves a hugely complex number of variables, and using this as an excuse for abandoning rigour and doing impressionistic opinion-mongering, then you can helpfully ask them in a loud, clear voice whether they've tried applying multidimensional stats, to find out what proportion of the variance in the data is accounted for by which variables. It can be even more gratifying for those who appreciate the suffering of an enemy to do those calculations yourself beforehand, and to demonstrate publicly that the underlying problem is in fact remarkably simple, and that just three of the variables account for 98% of the variance. A less gratifying prospect is to be asked in reply how you would propose to treat the eigenvectors, at which point you either bow out with some comment like 'Good point' if you've only read this book, or else get deep into a sadly technical debate which bores the pants off everyone if you've read some heavy-duty stats books as well.

Our other chapters have ended by introducing you to statistical tests related to the ones we've just covered. This time we'll travel to the further shores of research, describing not only statistical tests but also some complementary approaches from other disciplines, which give an excuse to bring in the story about the Russian tanks a bit later on.

Beyond statistics: approaches related and complementary to multidimensional statistics

Multidimensional statistics are useful for finding underlying patterns in your data. There are, however, other ways of finding underlying regularities in your data. Why should you care? One good reason is that the other ways are based on different foundations from those used for multidimensional statistics, so you can use them to tackle some questions and problems (not all, but some . . .) that multidimensional statistics can't handle. The next sections give very brief descriptions of other methods which could be used much more widely.

Data mining

This is an umbrella term which covers a variety of approaches (including multidimensional statistics). **Data mining** is quite widely used in industry, often for finding regularities in customers' buying behaviour, and was developed for handling extremely large data sets (for instance, sales figures for hundreds of thousands of customers and millions of purchases). There's a well-established data mining community, and a well-established set of approaches and range of software which they use, so if you're planning to tackle a particularly big data set, then it would be worth considering data mining as a way of tackling it.

Machine learning

Machine learning is also an umbrella term; it covers various ways of using software to identify regularities and patterns in data. Some of these ways involve statistics, but others don't – some machine learning systems are able to handle purely qualitative data. An example of this would be taking qualitative data about different species of insects, and getting the machine learning system to find possible ways of dividing those species into clusters based on qualitative characteristics (e.g. their preferred lifestyle) rather than their Linnaean classification by genus and species. Similarly, you might be able to use a machine learning system to find regular sequences of interactions between individuals – for instance, 'In the transcripts of these conversations, John only interrupts Angela if Chris has interrupted her first'.

Neural nets and genetic algorithms (including the story of the Russian tanks)

Neural nets (or **artificial neural networks**, to give them their full name) are pieces of software inspired by the way the human brain works. In brief, you can train a neural net to do tasks like classifying images by giving it lots of examples, and telling it which examples fit into which categories; the neural net works out for itself what the defining characteristics are for each category. Alternatively, you can give it a large set of data and leave it to work out connections by itself, without giving it any feedback. There's a story, which is probably an urban legend, which illustrates how the approach works and what can go wrong with it. According to the story, some NATO researchers trained a neural net to distinguish between photos of NATO and Warsaw Pact tanks. After a while, the neural net could get it right every time, even with photos it had never seen before. The researchers had gleeful visions of installing neural nets with miniature cameras in missiles, which could then be fired at a battlefield and left to choose their own targets. To demonstrate the method, and secure funding for the next stage, they organised a viewing by the military. On the day, they set up the system and fed it a new batch of photos. The neural net responded with apparently random decisions, sometimes identifying NATO tanks correctly, sometimes identifying them mistakenly as Warsaw Pact tanks. This did not inspire the powers that be, and the whole scheme was abandoned on the spot. It was only afterwards that the researchers realised that all their training photos of NATO tanks had been taken on sunny days in Arizona, whereas the Warsaw Pact tanks had been photographed on grey, miserable winter days on the steppes, so the neural net had flawlessly learned the unintended lesson that if you saw a tank on a gloomy day, then you made its day even gloomier by marking it for destruction.

That's a bit of a lengthy digression, but the underlying point is an important one in relation to statistics as well as machine learning. If you don't really understand how the software or statistical test is doing something, then there's always the risk that you'll get a very convincing-looking output which is in fact ludicrously wrong.

Genetic algorithms

Genetic algorithms are bits of software modelled explicitly on Darwinian evolution. Like neural nets, they can be trained to find patterns by themselves; unlike neural nets, you can actually do the equivalent of lifting the lid and seeing what they're getting up to. They work by taking a number of variables which you specify, and then randomly generating dozens of combinations between them. For instance, you might tell the genetic algorithm about the age, height and place of birth of each subject, together with their performance in the high jump, and then ask the genetic algorithm to find out the best combination of predictors for high jump performance. The genetic algorithm will then generate lots of random combinations for the variables, ranging from apparently silly combinations such as subtracting age in years from height in centimetres through to more sensible-looking ones. It next sees how each of these combinations performs at predicting the answer for each of the training examples you give it. It then throws away the combinations which perform worst, but keeps the best-performing combinations; the cunning bit is that it also takes chunks from each of the best-performing combinations and splices these together to form new combinations (which is where the bit about Darwinian evolution comes in). You then repeat the cycle numerous times. Usually the system performs badly in the first few cyles, then improves steadily until it reaches a point where it's not improving any more; that's where you usually stop. At their best, genetic algorithms can perform significantly better than human experts in tasks involving lots of combinations of variables – for instance, finding the best shape and angle for propellor blades. Often, the outcomes are demonstrably better than any pre-existing solution, but radically different from what a human would have thought of (for instance, asymmetric propellors). A great advantage of this approach is that you can check what it's getting up to by simply looking at the rules that it's using: if you see a rule along the lines of 'if the picture is bright, then the tank is friendly' then you can see the potential flaw immediately.

By this point, statistics might be losing their novelty for you, so the next chapter wraps things up, and the book then stops.

12

Some general considerations

Nuts and bolts • Statistical issues • Theoretical musings • Closing thoughts

> *[This] will conclude the terrible business we have been going through ... but I'm afraid it won't set your mind at rest unless I expressly assure you how very conclusive it is.*
>
> (*The Case of Charles Dexter Ward*, p. 296)

This chapter brings together various themes which cropped up in assorted places throughout the book. It's divided into three main parts. The first deals with low-level nuts and bolts: classic ways of making your life easier and of reducing the risk of disaster. The second deals with higher-level statistical issues. The third contains some theoretical musings, which you might find useful as inspiration for the discussion section of your write-up, if you're a student doing a final-year or master's project (though if so, you might wish to remember that your markers may well have read this book, so you should proceed with due tact).

Nuts and bolts

Working neatly is something which can make your life much, much easier at a time when it really matters, such as the day before the deadline for handing in your project write-up. If you keep your data tidily organised and clearly laid out, then it's much easier to make sense of it at the end. There's a horrible temptation, when you're in the middle of data collection, to slap the numbers down quickly, which might save a bit of time then, but which will sow the seeds of later grief when you're trying to work out whether a key bit of data should read '128' or '728' and you can't decipher your own scrawl. Some commendable students prepare neatly customised sheets for their data; this has the further advantage that these sheets will look virtuous if you include an example in the appendix of your write-up. If your study includes a pilot study, to test out your methods, then the pilot study is usually a good opportunity to try out ways of recording and storing your data.

It's also an extremely good idea to back up your data and to keep a copy off-site, so that you don't end up with the copy burning companionably next to the original data in the smouldering ruins of your home. A related point is that it's wise to photocopy your raw data and then do any processing (annotation, marginal totals, etc.) on the photocopies rather than the originals, so if anything goes wrong in your analysis you haven't irrevocably scruffed up your master copy. For some purposes, such as writing notes to yourself in the margins, it can be useful to use different colours of ink to make it clear which bits were written when (e.g. final checks versus pre-final checks).

How long do you keep your raw data for? Different disciplines have different conventions, if you're a professional researcher – it's typically 5–7 years. The reason for keeping it is that if anyone accuses you of fraud (or, as more often happens, one of your past collaborators is accused of fraud) you can produce your raw data and demonstrate your innocence. In some fields, this is hardly ever an issue, but in others there are well-established regulations about it. It's mentioned because some students do work good enough to be published, usually with their supervisor, and it can put you both in a difficult position if your supervisor discovers after publication of your article that you have cheerfully destroyed the raw data.

Double-checking all numbers is standard best practice; even the most meticulous people make mistakes. The best way to do this is by working in different directions – for instance, if you're adding a list of numbers, add them from top to bottom the first time, and then check them by adding from bottom to top. This reduces the risk that you'll make the same mistake the second time. If you're using a spreadsheet to do this, then double-check that your formulae and macros are all correctly set up – it's horribly easy to make a mistake, especially if you're cutting-and-pasting.

Doing sanity checks is highly advisable. This was probably easier to do in the days before computers, since you would have to work directly with the raw numbers, and you were likely to spot if something looked a bit dodgy. It's a good idea to eyeball your raw data before doing anything with it: this means simply looking at the raw data, to check whether any of the values look like potential misprints. For instance, if your subjects are schoolchildren, and one of the entries for 'age' reads '41' then this is almost certainly a misprint, possibly for '14'. If this happens, you need to go back to the original source of this information and find out the correct value – it's not safe simply to guess that the value should be 14 and to amend it. If you can't verify the correct figure, then you'll need to exclude the data for that subject, with some phrasing along the lines of: 'one subject was excluded from the analysis because of incomplete data'. If you're entering your data into a software package, you'll need to check that it's gone in correctly – even if your original hard copy records were correct, you might have miskeyed something when typing it into the machine, and if your raw data were entered directly into your laptop, there's still the small but real chance that the reading-in of the data file into the stats package mangled something.

In addition to sanity-checking the original data, you need to check that you know how to use your statistical test correctly. The best way of doing this is usually to take a textbook and work out the answer to one of its examples; if you get the correct answer, you can then proceed confidently to use the test on your own data. This is particularly advisable if you're using a software stats package. The software is unlikely to make any mistakes in calculation, but fallible human beings often press the wrong buttons and choose the wrong options, resulting in the software doing the wrong calculations.

A final sanity check is to look at the results, and see if they make sense. For example, if you have two smallish groups of subjects with almost identical scores, and your software claims that there is a statistically significant difference between them, then it would be a good idea to check that you did the test correctly.

Layout and **abbreviations** are issues which probably won't cause you to lose much sleep until the closing stages of your write-up, when you suddenly discover the problems involved in fitting your tables onto the page size on which The System insists. You may be allowed to use fold-out A3 tables, but in most institutions you're usually stuck with A4, which is just about big enough for small to medium data sets, but only just. At this point you may discover one of the reasons why so many publications brutishly depersonalise the human participants by turning them into cursory numbers: 's1' lets you get away with narrower columns than 'participant JH'. (There's also the consideration that anonymising them to 's1' reduces the chances of your being sued to hell and back if you accidentally use their real initials, and someone works out which of the people in your study of unethical behaviours was the one who stole the tea money.) Similarly, you may be pathetically grateful for the extra space you can claw back by writing a sigma (Σ) rather than 'total'. It's a good idea to look carefully at some tables in professional arenas such as journal articles, and see how they save space; it might save you a lot of grief. Similarly, it's worth persevering with the symbols, since they can both save you space and earn you brownie points. To help with this process, Table A.1 in the Appendix gives a list of common symbols and abbreviations.

Statistical issues

Choosing the right test is probably the most serious source of error when using statistics. The wise way to tackle this is to sweet-talk a statistician at the earliest stages of planning your research. There's a good chance not only that you will be told what the right test is for your needs, but also that you'll get some useful advice about a better research design which will let you get more out of your data for less effort. Statisticians are rarely asked for help at this stage, when their advice is most useful; usually, they're pestered by people with a boxful of data collected via an unspeakable research design. It's occasionally possible to salvage something from the squalid results, but usually the 'boxful of data' experience ends in gloom for all concerned. This is why statisticians are likely to be much more welcoming and helpful if you approach them at the outset.

What happens if you can't find a friendly statistician? One way is to work through the decision tree that appears in almost every stats book. If you make the right choice at each branch in the tree, then this will give you the right answer; unfortunately, beginners often (by definition) don't know enough to be sure of choosing the correct branch, and end up in error. Another solution, which avoids this risk, is to use a research design based directly on a reputable source, and to use the same type of statistical analysis as this template. If, for instance, your project involves an extension of a study recently published in a journal, then you may well be able to use the same research design and the same stats as that study. This approach has obvious advantages, but some less obvious risks. One is that the original study might itself be using the wrong statistical test – a depressingly high proportion of published studies even in reputable sources use the wrong test. Another is that you might have introduced a subtle change in your design which means that you can't use the same stats test as the original study used.

If all of the above fail, then the Right Thing is to err on the side of caution by using a conservative test. The usual suspects here are **Spearman's test** if you're doing correlations and **chi-squared** if you're testing for differences between groups.

One-tailed and **two-tailed tests** are, strictly speaking, to do with research design and the quality of your moral fibre rather than statistics. In classical times, the oracle at Delphi used two main strategies when predicting the future. Usually the priests, who had excellent sources of information, could make a good informed guess about the answer to a question. If they couldn't make a good informed guess, then they would use a phrasing which vindicated them regardless of outcome. The most famous example of this was when they told a Persian emperor that if he invaded Greece, a great empire would be destroyed; they didn't mention which empire it would be, and duly reaped the credit when the destroyed empire turned out to be his own, rather than the

Greek empire which he had in mind. You can do just the same in research design, by predicting that there will be a difference between the two groups you are studying: if you do this, then you can claim the credit if group A performs better than group B, and also claim the credit if the opposite happens and group B performs better than group A.

As you might suspect, this doubles your chances of being right. As you might also suspect, this affects the scores that you need to reach on your statistical test before you can say that results are statistically significant. If you predict the direction of the difference, then it's known as a one-tailed test; if you don't predict the direction, and just say that there will be a difference in one direction or the other, then it's known as a two-tailed test. If you're doing a two-tailed test, then you need to treat the results from your stats test as being twice as likely as for a one-tailed test. Suppose, for instance, that you predicted that group A would perform better than group B; this is a case for a one-tailed test, because you're predicting the direction of the difference. You perform the test, and reach significance at the 0.05 level. If, however, you had simply predicted that one group would perform differently from the other, then you would perform the same statistical test with the same data, and at the end you would double the significance level that came out. In this example, that would give you a p value of 0.10, which is not statistically significant.

The obvious temptation is to see what result comes out, and then pretend that this is the outcome you were predicting, so you could use the more powerful one-tailed test. Suppose, for instance, that you're an archaeologist and that one of your diggers tells you they've found several cows' thigh bones in the Iron Age pit that they're excavating, with all the bones being from the same side of the animals. Having had a classical education, you wonder whether this might be related to a Celtic custom of treating the right thigh as the hero's portion, and you look forward to using a one-tailed test on the data. This hope is brutally dashed at tea-break, when the digger mentions that the thighs were all from the left leg, not the right leg. What might you be tempted to do? One possibility would be to look for some obscure classical or legendary reference to using the left legs for some ritual purpose such as curses (or to claim that they're the legs which the heroes didn't eat); this would then allow you to do a one-tailed test in the opposite direction.

As this example demonstrates, there's a grey ethical area involved – it's not always easy to say where blatant opportunism ends and brilliant new insight begins. The usual convention, as ever, is to err on the side of conservatism, unless your research question clearly points towards only one possible prediction. It's important to note that this isn't the same as setting out to prove something, which is doomed to end in tears sooner or later. One of the studies on which I once worked involved a very clear one-tailed prediction based on the literature; when that prediction turned out to be spectacularly wrong, this showed that the literature wasn't covering the whole problem, and led to some very fruitful research as the consequence of this significant absence of statistically significant result.

Theoretical musings

Statistics are not just about calculations; they're also about a way of thinking, and a way of tackling research questions. An example of this relates to how you phrase your research hypothesis so that it links up with an appropriate test.

Hypothesis phrasing and integration with tests sounds impressive, which is often a useful attribute to have. What it means in this context is that if you can tackle your research question from a direction which allows you to use statistics properly, then this gives you a lot of power. You're able to identify which possible answers are in fact unlikely to be correct, and to identify those which are a better match with the evidence. You're able to answer the 'so what?' question by giving a figure for the odds against a given possibility. You can do a lot of other things too, as a thoughtful reading of some research papers involving statistics will demonstrate.

The phrase about 'a direction which allows you to use statistics properly' is the key phrase here. Inferential statistics produce an answer which is phrased in terms of probabilities; to use inferential statistics properly, you therefore need to learn the art of phrasing a research question where the appropriate answer is a probability. There are various effective ways of doing this, which are described in devoted depth by books on research methods. You might, for instance, ask a question such as: 'Are there significantly more sub-plots in the work of Shakespeare than in the work of Jeffrey Archer?' This is something you can test statistically, by counting the number of sub-plots for each author, and then running the appropriate test on them. If there is a statistically significant difference, then you have some evidence which is more than just subjective opinion about the relative styles of the two authors; if there is no statistically significant difference, then that tells you something interesting too – it would be a significant absence of a difference, in relation to most critics' perceptions of these authors.

In some disciplines, there's a long-established tradition of thinking this way; in others, it's unheard of. A common accusation is that research with statistics suffers from the law of implementation: just as a small boy with a hammer tends to view everything as needing to be hammered, so research with statistics tries to force every shape of problem into the same shape of hole. A common counter-accusation is that people who claim this are trying to conceal their inability to do sums, and don't really understand how empirical research works. I have no great desire to get dragged into this debate, having quite enough other things to do with my life, but it's worth mentioning as a parting thought that there are a lot of research areas which are suitable for research using statistics, but where this approach has not been properly tried so far.

Abuse of statistics has been around for as long as statistics (though in fairness, dodgy reasoning and abuse of anecdotal evidence have been equally deep sources of moral failure for much longer). Some abuse is unintentional, due to honest misunderstanding; some is intentional, and due to sin of various sorts, with money and ideology often visible among the prime suspects. This is one of the reasons why systematic research using statistics is closely linked with the idea of looking at the whole problem space, and methodically reducing it by eliminating candidate explanations one by one. With this approach, you're using statistics within a big picture, so your readers should be able to see the context of your findings. This is in contrast to most of the improper uses of statistics, which typically involve taking one or two findings out of context, without the big picture.

Closing thoughts

Beowulf ends on a dramatic note, with the hero's funeral mound on its headland, against the night sky; the original release of *Blade Runner* has a strong, sombre real ending, with the protagonists fleeing to an unknown future, but then tacks on a cheerier bit, demanded by the producers to increase the box-office sales; *Leningrad Cowboys Go America* simply stops. It would be pleasant to do a *Beowulf*, but by this stage in the writing process my dramatic powers are worn a bit thin, so rather than tack on an iffy ending, this book will do a *Leningrad Cowboys* and just stop. I hope you've found it useful and enjoyable.

Appendix

Some useful symbols • Interpretations

But this curve is a complicated one, and its full mathematical treatment is too hard for us.

(On Growth and Form, p. 58)

Some useful symbols

If you haven't been through a classical education, then the number of exotic-looking symbols used in maths might appear a bit bewildering. It's worth persevering with them, though, because (a) they can save a lot of space when you're creating a fiddly table and don't have much room, (b) they can be useful as a shorthand for labelling things when the use of numbers or ordinary letters would be confusing, and (c) using the correct symbol is usually good for an extra brownie point when your work is being marked, which might just be the brownie point that tilts things in your favour. Table A.1 shows some symbols that you might find useful, and includes a few notes and comments which might help you to remember them more easily.

TABLE A.1 Some useful symbols

Symbol	Name	Notes
Σ	sigma	Capital 'S' in Greek. Used as abbreviation for 'sum', i.e. total.
σ	sigma	Lower-case 's' in Greek. Used for the standard deviation in your sample.
$\sigma - 1$	sigma – 1	Lower-case 's' in Greek, minus 1. Used for the population standard deviation.
n	n	Symbol for the number of things in your sample, as in '$n = 32$'.
α	alpha	Greek 'a'. Used quite widely in maths and related fields when you want to give something a temporary name; Greek beta and gamma (described below) are also often used for this.
β	beta	Greek 'b'.
γ	gamma	Greek 'g' (third letter in the Greek alphabet).
δ	delta	Greek 'd' (fourth letter in the Greek alphabet)
ε	epsilon	Greek 'e' (fifth letter in the Greek alphabet).
χ^2	chi-squared	chi is a Greek letter (22nd in the alphabet), pronounced 'ky' (rhymes with 'sky'). Chi-squared is the name of a non-parametric test.
ρ	rho	Greek 'r'; pronounced like 'roe'. Spearman's rho is a statistical test.

Interpretations

Table A.2 explains some of the phrases commonly used by Bad People when they are doing sinful things with statistics. You should be aware of these phrases so that you do not inadvertently use them yourself and give the wrong impression.

TABLE A.2 Things Bad People say

They say:	This means:
an increase of up to 78%	One of my results was this high; the rest were nowhere near this level.
300% increase in membership over the last 12 months	Our club had two members last year, and now it has six.
our fast-growing club	Our club had two members last year, and now it has six members, so it has tripled in size, which is pretty fast-growing, isn't it?

300% increase	Three times as big as the number we started with. Statisticians tend to describe this as an increase of 200%, i.e. twice the number you started with, added to the number you started with.
200% decrease	What this means is usually anyone's guess – strictly speaking, it would mean that you're now dealing with negative numbers. Usually it appears to mean 'a very big decrease'.
85.7% of people sampled	Six out of the seven people sampled.
a random sample	I asked a few people who happened to be conveniently available and who didn't look too scary.
an average of 73%	Whichever meaning of 'average' best suits my case.
a mean of 73%	A mean dragged in the direction I want by a bizarre outlier which I don't propose to mention.
a mode of 73%	Two of my 38 respondents happened to produce the result I wanted; I'm not planning to mention the other results, which were scattered in a way that I'd rather not talk about.
a median of 73%	A nice sensible-looking figure which doesn't hint at the wild extremes in the data, which I'd rather not talk about.
a sample of 23,427 people	A very big sample, which will allow me to inflate my p values in the direction I want.
a representative sample	(Usually) an unrepresentative sample.
a representative sample	(Sometimes) a sample which really is representative, and for which I plan to claim every possible bit of credit.
reliable	(Usually) valid.
valid	(Usually) reliable.

Bibliography

This bibliography is intended to introduce some good representative texts and some classics that my colleagues and I have found useful. As you will probably have gathered by now, disciplines differ in the types of problems that they have to deal with, and in the statistics which are most suitable for those problems. I've included a couple of examples of medical statistics books and of statistics books for psychologists, but life's too short to include examples of statistics books for all the disciplines which academia has spawned. Where there isn't an accompanying comment about a book, this simply means that the book does what it says in the title and that no further comment is needed. If you feel a desire to find more good stats books, there is unlikely to be a shortage of them in the foreseeable future, and the nearest friendly statistician (or an Internet search on "introduction statistics") will give you enough reading to keep you occupied for years.

Altman, D. (1991). *Practical Statistics for Medical Research*. London: Chapman & Hall/CRC.

Brace, N., Kemp, R. and Snelgar, R. (2006). *SPSS for Psychologists: A Guide to Data Analysis using SPSS for Windows* (3rd edition). London: Palgrave.
SPSS is one of the most commonly used statistical packages; this edition of the book deals with versions 12 and 13 of SPSS, and there will probably be other editions as further versions of SPSS are released. As the title suggests, this book is primarily about SPSS rather than about statistics, but it's a very useful guide to the package.

Campbell, M.J. and Machin, D. (1999). *Medical Statistics: A Commonsense Approach*. New York: John Wiley & Sons.

Chatfield, C. (1995) *Problem Solving: A Statistician's Guide*. London: Chapman & Hall.
A really good book on how to do research in conjunction with statistics, rather than just on statistics.

Clegg, F. (1982). *Simple Statistics: A Course Book for the Social Sciences*. Cambridge: Cambridge University Press.
This book takes a humorous approach, with numerous cartoons. Some readers love the cartoons; others don't; if you do love them, this may be the book to take you further into statistics.

Field, A. (2005). *Discovering Statistics Using SPSS* (2nd edition). London: Sage.
This is about statistics and SPSS, rather than just about SPSS.

Green, J. and d'Oliveira, M. (2006). *Learning to Use Statistical Tests in Psychology* (3rd edition). Maidenhead: Open University Press.
A good example of a book about using statistics within a discipline, as opposed to a book about statistics.

Griffith, A. (2007). *SPSS for Dummies*. Hoboken, NJ: John Wiley & Sons.
A humorous, accessible introduction to SPSS, one of the most widely used statistics packages.

Hays, W. L. (1988). *Statistics* (4th edition). New York: Holt, Rinehart & Winston.
A classic statistics reference book.

Hogg, R.V. and Tanis, E.A. (2005). *Probability and Statistical Inference* (7th edition). London: Prentice Hall.
A book widely recommended for first- and second-year maths students, which supplies the theory behind the tests if you want to get deeper into how statistics actually work.

Howitt, D. and Cramer, D. (2005). *Introduction to Statistics in Psychology* (3rd edition). Harlow: Pearson.

Huff, D. (1991) *How to Lie with Statistics*. London: Penguin.
A clear, entertaining, classic guide to descriptive statistics.

Rumsey, D. (2003). *Statistics for Dummies*. Hoboken, NJ: John Wiley & Sons.
An amusing, irreverent and comprehensive introductory guide to statistics.

Siegal, A.F., and Morgan, C. J. (1996) *Statistics and Data Analysis: An Introduction*. New York: John Wiley & Sons.
A good book for students who feel nervous about statistics; it has plenty of examples and accessible explanations.

Weiss, N. (2007). *Introductory Statistics* (8th edition). Harlow: Pearson.
A good introductory book.

Glossary and useful concepts

This isn't a complete glossary, since the usual statistical terms are explained in the text and can be found via the Index. Instead, this section focuses on some useful concepts which you might not find in more formal books, and on some standard concepts which are particularly often misunderstood.

Arbitrary Chosen without any compelling reason; haphazard. This is not the same as 'random'. For instance, you might select an arbitrary sample of authors whose surname begins with 'M'. This will not be random, since you'll end up with a disproportionate number of Scottish authors whose surnames begin with 'Mac' or 'Mc'. A classic error is to claim you're using a random sample when you're actually using an arbitrary one.

Bad People A lot of the conventions in statistics and in research are reactions to sins committed by people in the Past. The phrase 'Bad People' is a convenient shorthand for this.

Cynical Readers People marking your work (if you're a student) or reviewing your work (if you're a researcher) will usually have encountered Bad People, and will therefore be wary about giving you the benefit of the doubt if you've done something questionable.

Data Many academics are aware that this word is the plural of 'datum' and means 'given things'. Many academics therefore treat it like any other self-respecting plural, and use phrasings like 'these data are . . .'. Other academics treat it like a singular, and use phrasings such as 'this data is . . .'. You get more pedantry points for treating it as a plural. Whichever phrasing you use, it's likely to irritate people of the other persuasion. You can usually dodge round this by using careful phrasing such as 'these findings' or 'the results' or verbs which are the same in the singular and plural, such as 'can' and past tenses.

Dice Dice are widely used as examples in statistics. The word 'dice' is agreed by everyone to be the correct plural form. There are, however, two schools of thought about what the correct singular form is. Academics teaching stats courses are normally well aware that the pedantically correct singular form is 'a die'. Ordinary mortals tend to talk about 'a dice'. I've used 'a die'. Dice can be *loaded*, i.e. tampered with so that one face shows more often than the others, or *fair*, i.e. with each face showing equally often when thrown repeatedly. (The other possibility, that there's an accidental unevenness in their shape which results in one face showing more often than others, is not so often mentioned, but did occur in the old days, when manufacturing was less precise – some of the early probability theorists rolled real, actual dice thousands of times to measure probabilities, and we can tell from the results that their dice were slightly longer along one axis than along the others.)

Elder, Lauren The woman who survived a plane crash in the Sierra Nevada really did exist, and really did walk to civilisation, through snowdrifts, for thirty-six hours. With a broken arm. Wearing fashion boots with two inch heels. She climbed several thousand feet down a cliff in the process, for good measure.

Eyeballing the data Looking at the raw data to see if any patterns or trends are immediately obvious in it. This is a useful quick check in case you make some hideous mistake with the analysis later on – you'll probably spot the mistake quickly because it's different from what you're expecting from the eyeballing.

Facts (with a capital F) Ironic allusion to the belief that some disciplines (e.g. history) consist of indisputable, clear-cut facts. It's a wise idea to check where your data came from, if you're using historical data – just because it's neat and systematic, that doesn't mean it corresponds to reality.

Giggle test If you describe your research to knowledgeable colleagues and they giggle, then this suggests you may have done something silly and might want to reconsider some aspects of it.

Hypothetical Invented, fictitious, 'what if?'. Stats books often use hypothetical data, for the praiseworthy reasons that (a) this can be used to illustrate a point more clearly than real data, and (b) this saves the long-suffering writers from actually having to count, say, the instances of dramatic prefiguration in the minor novels of Barbara Cartland.

Last Tuesdayism The belief that the universe was created, complete with records, fossils and memories, last Tuesday. A classic example of an unfalsifiable belief – nobody can prove it wrong, but on the other hand it doesn't give you any useful insights into the nature of the universe and is therefore pretty pointless.

The Past Another ironic allusion. Many people have simplistic ideas about the Past; some people then elaborate these ideas into world-views which are based on dodgy foundations.

Sanity check A quick informal check that something is at least vaguely right, often performed by eyeballing the data or eyeballing the results from the statistical analysis. For instance, if your sanity check shows that the mean weight of the limpets you studied was 34.51 kilograms, then something has probably gone slightly wrong in your records or calculations.

The snowflake principle One snowflake is a tiny, fragile thing. The same snowflake accompanied by several thousand tons of other tiny fragile snowflakes in an avalanche is a very different proposition. A lot of statistical calculation is like this: composed of parts which are individually very easy, but which become a bit much in large quantities. (We're indebted to Peter McGeorge for this one.)

The Truth (with a capital T)   Yet another ironic allusion, to world-views which believe that only they are right, and that everyone who disagrees with them is wrong.

Sources of quotations at the beginning of each chapter

Darwin
By A. Desmond and J. Moore. Michael Joseph, London, 1991.

History of the Peloponnesian War
By Thucydides the Athenian, son of Olorus. Penguin, London, 1972 edition.

I Ching: The Book of Change
Translation by J. Blofeld, Unwin Paperbacks, London, 1985.

Master and Commander
By P. O'Brian. HarperCollins, London, 2002 edition.

On Growth and Form (abridged edition)
By D. W. Thompson. Cambridge University Press, Cambridge, 2006.

The Dreams in the Witch-House
By H.P. Lovecraft. In *H.P. Lovecraft Omnibus 1: At the Mountains of Madness*. Grafton
Books, London, 1989.

The Case of Charles Dexter Ward
By H.P. Lovecraft. In *H.P. Lovecraft Omnibus 1: At the Mountains of Madness*. Grafton
Books, London, 1989.

Index